DEER CAMP

An American Tradition

True Stories of an Old-Fashioned Deer Camp
The Pine Hill Club

1st Edition

Mills Publications

Published by
MILLS PUBLICATIONS
576 Hiawatha Drive
Mt. Pleasant, MI 48858

All photos by the author unless otherwise credited
Cover photo by Robert C. Mills
Cover and page design by Richard Rae

Printed in the United States of America

First Edition

Library of Congress Cataloging-in-Publication Data

Mills, Robert © 2001
    Deer Camp — An American Tradition / Robert C. Mills — 1st ed.

Includes bibliographical references and appendices
ISBN 0-9712660-0-X
1. Deer Camp — North America. 1. Title.

To my father, grandfather, uncles and sons
who each in his own way taught me to
sit quietly, walk slowly and shoot straight.

With their help I have become a seasoned deer hunter

My love to all.

Robert C. Mills

ACKNOWLEDGEMENTS

The list of people to thank for this book is truly endless.

First and foremost, I want to thank my father Clayton H. Mills for providing me with the opportunity to enjoy and appreciate the great out-of-doors. Dad was a tireless mentor and coach. He taught me an appreciation for nature and the joy of the deer camp and the hunt. Dad truly loved to trap muskrat, mink and raccoon. As a young boy I followed him for many miles while checking his traps. Together, we spent hours skinning, stretching and drying what he had trapped. He developed in me an appreciation for the land. My father was always patient, jovial and honest. He taught me to shoot straight and never give up on a wounded deer. He also taught me great respect for the animals in their natural environment.

I must also express appreciation to my grandfather Harry Mills for letting me use his .22 rifle and 12 gauge shotgun, when I didn't have a gun of my own. My Uncle Vern Mills, who was my regular and steady deer-hunting partner for many years, taught me to have fun in a deer camp. His ever-present smile would light up the woods and his laugh was contagious for all to enjoy.

Thanks and appreciation must also be extended to my hunting partner and friend Alan Quick. For 30 years we have hunted the mighty whitetail buck. Al has always been a great supporter of conservation and all the good things a deer camp portrays. Al is one of my closest hunting friends.

Dr. Roger Dixon, longtime camp member, taught me that killing is only a small part of the joy of a deer camp. He tirelessly edited this book and contributed many ideas and tips for successful hunting over the years. Roger is a committed bow hunter and a highly respected colleague, friend and member of the Pine Hill Club.

I must also thank my wife Marge, who has always been most supportive of my deer hunting adventures. She sews buttons, helps pack my favorite woolens, and prepares the best camp chili and pies one could ever describe. Having a loving wife allows me to enjoy the woods without feeling guilty. She is also a great mother and outstanding cook. Our entire family enjoys the venison she so superbly prepares.

Finally, our four sons, Mike, Dave, Joe and Rick have allowed me to mentor, coach and share the skills I have learned from my father, grandfather and relatives. Their excitement at the deer camp and the pride they get from tagging a whitetail buck serves as a lasting memory of good times had by all.

Such unselfish and loving support from so many people has allowed me to pursue my passion of deer hunting.

Thanks to all!

C ONTENTS

INTRODUCTION

*M*y goal in writing this book, *DEER CAMP — An American Tradition,* is to capture in print some of the varied experiences shared by hunters in pursuit of the greatest game animal in the world — the Whitetail Buck.

How does one capture the excitement of the hunt, the joy of a young hunter's first deer, the smell of bacon frying or the glow of a warm campfire? The best way is to "tell it like it is" and that's what this book is designed to record.

Special sections will highlight techniques used by successful hunters, both young and old. In addition, chapters will be devoted to the best deer rifles and camp recipes. One chapter will highlight clothing and equipment selection. The bulk of the book will focus on true stories about our hunting camp — The Pine Hill Club.

Hundreds of years of combined hunting experiences will be captured in this volume. Both veteran and beginning hunters will enjoy reading about the events that occur in a deer camp. Deer hunting is truly an American tradition.

DEER CAMP — An American Tradition isn't just a location — it is a history!

I hope you enjoy the book.

Robert C. Mills

CHAPTER 1

Deer Camp — Early Beginnings

The Pine Hill Club era began in the summer of 1972!

While on a leisurely Sunday drive, Al Quick, a close personal friend and Director of Teacher Education at Central Michigan University, and I spotted a "For Sale" sign on a wooded piece of property in northwest Isabella County. The property was located near the town of Weidman, Michigan, approximately dead center in the middle of Michigan's mitten.

After contacting the realtor, we walked the property. The land was slightly rolling. Tall aspen and stately oak trees lined two long ridges on either side of a lengthy swamp. This 80-acre property came complete with an old hand-operated water pump, remnants of a stone foundation from a mid-century homestead, and large pine trees guarding the entrance to the land.

Al and I noted abundant deer sign, jumped numerous partridge, and watched cottontails bound along an old fence left from turn of the century farming. There was no doubt this was a quality hunting spot! Within minutes after walking the land and briefly discussing the deal, we eagerly decided to purchase the property.

With the help of a local attorney, we closed the deal in a matter of days.

A written agreement helped define our partnership and spelled out terms of the purchase. The document also clearly delineated the operational guidelines for the joint venture.

With advice from legal counsel we spelled out every potential conflict we could envision before it occurred. We developed a written, signed agreement that would serve as our operational bylaws. Both Al and I were pleased with this agreement. For over 20 years of successful partnership, we never changed a single word!

Such a cornerstone agreement is absolutely essential for building a solid foundation between good friends who wish to enter into such a deer camp partnership. Nothing should be left to doubt!

Conceived in friendship and a joint love of the outdoors, the Pine Hill Club was born!

Growing from a common desire to own a few acres where we could hunt in safety, without competition from other hunters, the Pine Hill Club has become an institution in the area, far exceeding the original 80 acres and simple goals and desires Al and I shared that warm summer day.

This unique deer hunting camp has become a training ground for young hunters and a center of renewal for older sportsmen. Like a magnet, it annually draws scores of hunters from neighboring camps who share hunting stories and life experiences.

Both Al and I were ecstatic about our new purchase. We both knew that deer camps were the cornerstones of quality hunting and we made plans to ready the property for the upcoming fall hunt.

Then, as now, protection and development of the property for game management was a critical component of our stewardship. *"Managing the resource for future generations"* became our camp credo and it has served us well for the past three decades. Our grandchildren will be served by it, as well.

Together, we installed posts along the fence line and affixed the normal private property signs that designated the land as useable by the owners and their guests.

We added a gate by the driveway into the property and marked the boundary to the property with a single wire. As Robert Frost so sagely wrote, "Good fences make good neighbors."

In addition to posting and marking the property, we purchased 10,000 red pine and Scotch pine trees for spring planting. These plantings would be used to enhance the habitat and provide cover to all the different game species that abounded on the land.

I did not plan to actively hunt this property until our oldest son Mike reached the age of 14 — the age required in Michigan to legally rifle hunt. Also entering into my decision not to hunt the property at this time was a commitment I had made as caretaker/guide for the Willing Ranch. This property is a private hunting camp of nearly 3,000 acres, located in Gladwin County. For six years I had served as camp manager and would continue that commitment until Mike was old enough to hunt.

The Willing Ranch provided me a place to safely hunt and learn invaluable lessons about managing, hunting and tracking whitetail deer. I enjoyed working with the owner and the 50 members of this private hunting camp, where I received graduate training in deer management.

Selection of hunting spots on our newly purchased land became our next priority. Al chose three locations for hunting blinds. Two locations were along the oak ridge on the south side of the property, adjacent to the large east-west swamp dividing the land. Another blind was located in the birch trees on the north end of the land. Al's blind was located on one of the oak-lined ridges overlooking the swamp.

Al hunted the newly purchased property in the fall of 1972, accompanied by guests Tom Arch and Charles Pisoni. Both were professors from Central Michigan University and close mutual friends.

Al shot the first buck killed at the Pine Hill Club on the opening morning at 9:00 am. The deer was a large eight-pointer. We still have the mount in a place of honor on the wall of our cabin.

That initial eight-pointer was the first of hundreds of whitetail bucks harvested at the Pine Hill Club. Yearly records of the biggest buck killed at the camp since 1972 are listed in the appendix.

In the summer of 1974, our partnership purchased another contiguous 80 acres. Primarily comprised of cedar swamp and cattails, this new property helped provide food, cover and wintering habitat for the deer herd.

From this simple beginning, the Pine Hill Club has now grown to encompass 560 acres, plus an additional 200 acres of leased land.

Sole ownership was obtained in 1990 when I purchased Al's interest in the deer camp. Following that land purchase, an additional 80 acres of hunting property was added, as well as several building additions.

Al and I have continued to regularly hunt this outstanding deer haven, but we now share it with 19 other relatives and friends. Both Al and I strongly believe this is one of Michigan's best and most successful old-fashioned deer camps.

My First Hunting Season

The 1975 season marked the year our oldest son Mike would turn 14. As a result, I resigned my position as camp manager of the Willing Ranch and prepared to hunt with Al and Mike at the Pine Hill Club.

Mike was a good student, an enthusiastic outdoors person, and demonstrated an affinity for hunting deer. Being the oldest son, with three younger brothers, he was poised to be the first of the children to accept the challenge of the whitetail buck. His excitement, however, paled next to mine, as I prepared to experience both my first-born son's initiation into the very special world of the deer hunter and my first ever hunt at my own deer-hunting camp, the Pine Hill Club.

As noted, my wife, Marge, and I have four sons: Mike, Dave, Joe and Rick. Al and his wife, Arlene, have two sons: Geoff and Greg. Additionally, we both worked at Central Michigan University and our home life, like that of many young, working fathers, was constantly subject to interruptions by students needing help and other university obligations.

If we were going to truly bond with our sons and develop the special hunting atmosphere we wanted, it was quickly apparent we must leave our homes during deer season and have a sheltered camp from which to hunt and share experiences.

A Humble Creation

Therefore, during the summer of 1975, Al and I, with the help of our six young sons, began construction of a hunting cabin on our property. Our sons were near each other in age and had played together for years in the neighborhood where Al and I lived, only two blocks apart in a wooded area near Mt. Pleasant.

Calling this crude structure a "cabin" would be a compliment for this first shelter. It was a 12' x 16' building assembled in sections in my back yard. This small building had one door and four small windows. Construction clearly followed a low-budget format. Used windows, a donated door and rolled roofing kept expenses low.

Following construction, we diligently hauled the modular unit to the property. Floor, walls, roof trusses, boards and hardware for completion of the cabin were all transported to the site. Carefully, we assembled the building on cement blocks. This simple structure remains, to this day, the foundation of our deer camp lodge.

Heat was provided by a donated wood-burner. The wood stove would either roast you out or make you shiver depending on whether the fire had gone out or was roaring. Heat was determined by the setting on a damper embedded in the eight-inch metal stovepipe that protruded through the cabin ceiling.

A single propane Coleman lantern provided our lighting in 1975. We upgraded and installed a permanent propane light the next year. Water was hauled from the old hand pump, located about 100 yards from the cabin.

This little cabin provided the setting for many successful hunts and served as the base of camp operations until the first addition was constructed in 1979. Overall, five additions have been attached to the original small shelter to create today's lodge. As land was added to the camp, so were cabin additions.

That deer camp home, though small and crude, was always filled with laughter, stories, and memorable moments. The ever-present smell of wet socks, cigar-smoke and boot grease filled the air. Guests would often times open the door or the windows to clear the pungent air in the small structure.

This crowded, odor-filled creation perhaps best exemplifies the true beginning at the Pine Hill Club and our deer camp.

Annually, blaze orange clothes were piled high in the corners and hung on every available space. Well-oiled rifles, scarred by many years of use, rested on a crude gunrack nailed to the wall of the tiny cabin.

A small, apartment-size gas stove served to prepare meals. The oven, though hard to light, was a haven for added heat and drying wet socks, while baking biscuits, pies or other goodies.

In addition to the cabin, a buck pole was optimistically erected to hang deer harvested by the hunters. This buck pole was made from aspen trees cut from the property and the cross-member was held in place by a strong chain. The horizontal pole stood ten feet off the ground. Ample distance, we thought, to hang a full-bodied buck.

An old refrigerator was placed outside the cabin to protect food supplies from the many mice and squirrels that invaded the cabin. This refrigerator served to keep food cool in the summer and guarded the contents from freezing in the winter.

No electricity was available for the cabin. Because of this, no electrical appliances could be used. Therefore, coolers, lanterns, water jugs, and other camping essentials were used to store and protect basic supplies.

Venison liver with onions, fresh from the first day's hunt, quickly became a camp tradition. The cooking liver was prepared amidst a smoke-filled atmosphere of celebration as the successful hunters repeated stories of their kills.

On opening day all hunters looked forward to this meal. (Note, a recipe for cooking fresh deer liver is found in the section on camp recipes.)

Following a hearty meal of venison liver, onions, potatoes and baked goods, the hunters traditionally began an evening euchre tournament and teams challenged each other for the camp championship. Much joking and laughter occurred during these intense card games.

From the early beginnings of the camp, the card-playing rule has been that there could only be a maximum of $1 per game and $1 per euchre ventured in camp wagers. These numbers were spray painted on the cabin door as a visual reminder to all.

The bottom line is members are discouraged from risking any large sums of money. Legality aside, bets over a $1 often result in hard feelings among the losers and serve no valid purpose in a hunting camp.

(NOTE: Many hunting camps continue to endure loud arguments and hurt feelings from individuals losing large sums of money at games of chance. At the Pine Hill Club, members play cards for fun. No one gets serious about losing small amounts of money. Casinos are close by if anyone wishes to gamble seriously.)

Members enjoy a game of euchre and tall tales.

Small, crude and crowded, the cabin provided then, as now, an oasis from the reality of the outside world. Additionally, although not as important, it provided a haven for cold, wet, hunters returning from a day in the woods.

In the morning, filling the wood burner and lighting the propane lantern signaled the beginning of another day in the field. Arguments between the hunters over the best deer rifle, best hunting knife and largest buck sighted were ever-present subjects at the breakfast table.

With no telephone, electric lights, radio, television, newspaper or work schedules to contend with, the deer camp provided an environment for all to solve world problems, appreciate the beauties of nature, and to share very special experiences with our sons and friends.

Killing a buck became secondary to the importance of deer camp living. This fact remains as true today as it was nearly three decades ago!

Snoring commenced quickly on opening day night, within five minutes from lights out, and contests were generated between the hunters about who could snore the loudest. This was always a topic at the breakfast table, invoking laughter and good-natured kidding among the participants.

Over the years, as can be seen from the pictures elsewhere in the book, this simple structure has grown into two knotty pine-lined hunting lodges, where 21 members of the Pine Hill Club family sleep, eat, and participate in tall tales lived. However, no matter how large our camp grows, the memories of our early woods' home will always burn brightly.

Geraldine – Our Beloved Outhouse

Original camp members constructed a crude outhouse, dubbed "Geraldine" to serve their call-of-nature needs and to provide privacy and shelter from the rain and snow that befalls most deer camps during November.

Geraldine was constructed from plywood and two-by-fours and measured four feet by six feet. The structure included a two-hole seat to accommodate a duo of hunters. A tattered old deer head, also known as "Geraldine," complete with sunglasses, adorns the beloved outhouse wall.

Hunters commonly say they are going to visit Geraldine when the body moves them to take action.

Over the years we have added electric lights to the outhouse, as well as an eight-foot by six-foot addition, complete with sink and coatroom.

The addition of running water and a septic system, resulting in a modern bathroom in the lodge, has caused Geraldine to serve a reserve role at camp. However, she waits patiently for any overflow of hunters rushing to relieve themselves in the midst of a crowded indoor bathroom.

"Long live Geraldine" is a camp motto, spoken with deep appreciation by all the members, young and old.

The Biggest Buck

Five bucks were shot during the 1975-hunting season, including both Mike's first deer and the biggest buck ever harvested at the Pine Hill Club.

Dick Kolaja, my brother-in-law and an avid hunter who worked in an automotive factory in Flint, shot a magnificent twelve-pointer at 2:00 p.m. on opening day.

The huge buck startled Dick when it first appeared. He missed it with his first shot. However, it continued to run along a ridge adjacent to the wet swamp and Dick's blind. When the deer paused for a moment, a second shot from his Remington 721 bolt-action .300 Savage found its mark and the buck collapsed.

The buck had 12 massive points, with an outside spread of 24 inches. The dark-bodied deer was huge, scaling at 200 pounds after field dressing. It still remains the largest buck ever taken to date by any member at the Pine Hill Club.

That year my son Mike shot his first deer, a large spike-horn, with my Model 94 Winchester timber rifle. That deer was his first buck, but certainly not his last. He would repeat this feat many times over the years, although none would be as special as this initial deer.

In addition to Dick's 12-pointer and Mike's spike-horn, Al shot a four-point buck, Chuck Pisoni shot a nice eight-pointer behind the cabin, and I was able to hang a fat six-point buck. It was a very successful opening day for my first hunt at the Pine Hill Club, which grew to represent more about hunting and camaraderie than I ever imagined when Al and I first purchased the property.

This unique deer hunting camp has become a training ground for young hunters and center of renewal for older sportsmen. Like a magnet, it annually draws scores of hunters from neighboring camps who share hunting stories and life experiences.

Over the years, increasing numbers of hunting neighbors from area camps have visited the Pine Hill Club. A standing-room-only crowd often presents a setting of laughter, kidding, sharing and "one-upmanship" known only in a true deer camp. The first liar doesn't stand a chance is a frequent comment among the good-natured hunters.

Over the years, the small, simple, cabin structure has grown into two hunting lodges and a permanent buck pole, well worthy of the name. However, the memories of our early woods home are truly priceless.

Veteran members still talk about the rustic beginnings of the camp and how we survived in the crude facilities with no electricity, indoor plumbing or running water.

Regardless, those early days provided the cornerstone for the old-fashioned deer camp that still exists to this day.

Growing from a common desire to own a few acres where we could hunt in safety, without competition from other hunters, the Pine Hill Club has become an institution in the area, far exceeding the original

Pine Hill Club cabin.

dreams Al and I shared that memorable warm summer day when we first sighted the ground that would become the Pine Hill Club.

Over the years, untold numbers of young men have taken their first bucks under the tutelage of their fathers and other Pine Hill Club members. Based on a strong component of father-son memberships, the camp has dedicated itself to improving family relationships and building a strong love and respect for our outdoor world.

Hunters of all ages have shared their love of deer hunting and the wisdom they accumulated with others of this unique fraternity. If indeed it is true that a small percentage of the hunters take the vast majority of the deer year after year, our hunters are clearly among that select group. Sharing their knowledge not just with the young people of the camp, but with each other as well, they have created a very special hunting and family atmosphere that is indeed unique.

You will see, as you read this book, that after 30 years, the deer camp continues to provide laugher, good-natured debates, camaraderie and positive fellowship among the members. The smell of wood burning, boot grease, and liver and onions frying on opening night still remain as a reminder of days gone by in the camp.

From the crude beginning of the deer camp, traditions have been formalized. Throughout this book, I will share some of these, as well as successful hunting tips learned from years in the woods and favored camp recipes, plus some of the pranks and jokes played by the members.

Deer Camp — An American Tradition is a true story of deer hunting at its finest!

ENJOY!

Neighbor Keith Loomis stands by buck pole. Note coyote in picture.

CHAPTER 2

Membership in a Deer Camp

A safe hunting environment, designed around sound wildlife management principles and free from disruptive trespassers, is perhaps the single greatest attraction for hunters wishing to participate in a private deer camp. They are seeking a communion with nature without the challenge of sharing hunting space with any Tom, Dick, or Harry who might stumble into the woods.

Although Al and I originally purchased the Pine Hill Club property as a guaranteed safe hunting haven for our sons and ourselves, we quickly realized we needed to expand our vision for the future. We were blessed by having the opportunity to purchase the property and to share it with our sons; however, there is much more to deer hunting than just killing deer.

Mentoring for life, managing the resources we were given for future generations, and sharing life's experiences with kindred souls were unique opportunities we wished to make more available to our sons. If we limited the Pine Hill Club experiences to ourselves only, we would be ignoring a vast reservoir of knowledge that could be shared, not only with our children, but between ourselves as well.

Therefore, we made the decision to share our property with a few special friends, who held similar goals, founded on a love of nature's gifts. The Pine Hill Club was truly born as we began carefully opening the hunting and natural beauty of the woods to valued friends outside our immediate family. It was a decision that changed our lives and one we have never regretted. It also impacted the lives of many other individuals.

The membership of the Pine Hill Club is unique among most hunting camps. It is not composed of close family members, although the members maintain a very close personal relationship with each other, or of men with similar professional, religious or fraternal ties.

Teachers, college professors, a computer programmer, school superintendents, police detectives, plumbers, successful businessmen, a former mayor of a large Midwestern town, a career military man, college students, maintenance personnel, a metal fabrication expert, a building contractor, an engineer, and other diverse backgrounds are represented among the current membership.

Year after year, these men voluntarily give up weekends to participate in camp work days, readying the property for the upcoming season and improving the camp for use in the fall. They spend extensive time in the woods and at the camp during the fall seasons, ranging from a few days to weeks.

Each of these individuals has the opportunity to shoot deer outside the confines of the Pine Hill Club. Killing a deer is obviously not the primary motivating force stimulating them to share their time, their knowledge and their personal experiences with each other and their sons in this camp. Therefore, why do they do so?

Giving something back to nature is certainly a part of the appeal of the camp. For instance, each year members generate and share in wildlife management practices that enhance the habitat and provide cover, food and shelter for the game. These practices are described later and can serve as possible guidelines for sound conservation programs for similar deer camps, whether large or small.

Having a safe environment to hunt speaks for itself. Additionally, not having to worry about a strange hunter scenting up your hunting area, drinking alcoholic beverages in the woods, or scaring the deer coming down "your" runway all support the concept of club membership on private property.

Hunting the same environment year after year also provides camp members with a very special advantage: an ever-increasing knowledge of local deer movement and habits. Any hunter's chances for a successful hunt increase yearly with such an intimate understanding of the quarry and the habitat.

Membership in the Pine Hill Club, like in most other deer camps, is by invitation only. New members must be approved and confirmed by the owner/s. As in most deer camps, rules are clearly spelled out and new members are expected to follow these long established guidelines for operating the hunting camp.

The rules at the Pine Hill Club have not changed in nearly 30 years. They serve as foundation cornerposts to the membership in the use and care of the property. A copy of these rules is reproduced below for your review.

PINE HILL CLUB RULES

1. Use of the camp is by membership only. Members may use the property by paying fees and signing the Release of Liability Form.

2. Members may take their sons/daughters with them hunting. Non-members or relatives may not hunt, but may accompany the paying member. This activity is encouraged.

3. Only members may use the cabin during hunting season. (October 1st until January 1st. At other times families and guests may use facilities)

4. Hunters are assigned a hunting blind. No member has a "claim" on any specific hunting blind or hunting spot.

5. Hunters using the property for the opening two days of rifle deer season must agree to hunt all day. No walking during the first two days of season! Walking around the property interferes with other members.

---

6. *Safety first must be observed at all times! Know your target. No target practice is allowed during hunting season in the woods.*

7. *All DNR (Department of Natural Resources) rules must be observed! Guns must be in cases when in a vehicle, deer must be tagged properly, only legal game can be taken, hunter orange must be worn, and proper licenses are mandatory.*

8. *No member is allowed to trespass on property adjoining the Pine Hill Club. Violation may result in suspension of the membership.*

9. *Membership in the Pine Hill Club is by annual invitation. No non-members are permitted use of the property as guests without approval of the owner.*

10. *No alcohol is to be taken into the woods while hunting. Safety must be observed at all times. Guns/bows/arrows and alcohol do not mix!*

NOTE: Membership in the camp is a privilege and good sportsmanship is expected by all. New members will be selected after consulting with the current membership. Members who violate the above rules MAY LOSE their membership. Suggestions for making the deer camp better are welcomed and encouraged.

Much like the original partnership agreement, these rules form the bedrock for the operation of our private deer camp. Hunters who violate the guidelines or demonstrate disrespect for fellow hunters or the game should be — and are — dropped from the camp.

An unwritten rule of the camp also includes having a positive, friendly attitude. Complainers, gripers, and negative people contribute little. They nibble at the lettuce of the soul of a successful hunting camp. Potential members such as these rarely make it through by the screening process. If they do, an immediate attitude adjustment is required or they are not invited back the following year.

In respect to membership, heavy emphasis is placed on father/son combinations. Over half of our current membership consists of father/son combinations.

Many members have over 25 years experience in the deer camp. They have become like family and many view each other as "brothers" or "uncles."

A strong bond exits between the members, who consider the camp family as a "circle of steel," meaning they are strongly bound together, not only in a common love of deer hunting, but through a camaraderie based on mutual respect and brotherhood.

Social and professional status is dropped at the camp gate. Members become one fraternity, sharing a common bond involving the love of the woods and the fair chase pursuit of whitetails.

A long standing list of "WAN-A-BE" Pine Hill Club members exists and serves as the conduit for replacing the rare vacancy in our hunting club.

Death, over the years, has claimed some members, who will always be fondly remembered and missed at the camp.

Camp members share in all the sundry chores of a deer camp, including cooking, dishes, and carrying wood for the fireplace, as well as dragging deer from the woods and processing venison.

Additionally, members are expected to participate in two work days per year. The work days involve cutting wood, painting, and general camp repairs to prepare the physical facilities for the upcoming season.

These events occur annually in the spring. Renewed friendship, light-hearted kidding, and reliving past deer kills — and the occasional miss — highlight these days. Work days are always a type of celebration and a special bonding occurs among the hunters during these occasions.

Members are also encouraged to offer suggestions and contribute ideas designed to make the camp better. Lessons in leadership can be learned in owning and operating a deer camp. Believe me, I speak from experience.

First, you can't have 21 people making decisions. Secondly, without focus and organization, the system will collapse. Without leadership focused on the goals of the camp, the system will deteriorate into arguments, differences of opinion, and hurt feelings.

Other common sense guidelines make the operation of the hunting

Bill Waters prepares eggs for camp breakfast on opening morning.

camp a positive, bonding experience for the members. For instance, although mostly unwritten, the following operational procedures have developed over the years at the Pine Hill Club.

1. *Never leave the cabin unlocked or messy. The member who next visits camp won't appreciate a dirty cabin or clean-up chores you left behind.*

2. *Security is always a constant. Lock the doors and shut the windows when you leave the cabin. Close all the gates and secure them with the locks provided for this purpose.*

3. *Don't trespass off club property, unless you are tracking a wounded deer. If you trespass, without cause, you invite neighbors to do the same. (Note: Each year, I visit adjoining property owners and share this rule. While neighbors are welcome to follow a blood trail onto Pine Hill Club property, they are not welcome to trespass!)*

4. *Don't bring a guest to HUNT without permission. (Guests are allowed but cannot hunt without the owner's permission.) Paying members deserve the right to a private deer camp.*

5. *No alcohol is ever allowed in the woods. Weapons and alcohol do not mix. Drinking should be confined to the cabin. Never, never drink when hunting. (Only once in 30 years have we lost a member due to an infraction of this rule. That was once too often!)*

6. *Don't shoot a deer unless you can use it. Indiscriminant killing of deer is not allowed! This rule is strictly enforced.*

7. *Shooting of fawns and button bucks is not allowed! If a mistake happens, members must report it to the owner. (At the Pine Hill Club, we shoot only mature deer. Bucks must have six points or more.)*

The development of common sense, mutually acceptable rules is critical to operating a successful deer camp. Such guidelines allow for harmony and respect for game, the land and the rights of other members. Our rules have served the membership well at the Pine Hill Club.

Members at the Pine Hill Club are very accepting of these fundamental guidelines. They enjoy a safe, friendly hunting environment, based on valid wildlife management practices, free from disruptive trespassers. Our written, as well as unwritten rules, enhance the joy of our deer camp by spelling out member expectations in advance of possible problems. Anyone wishing to organize a successful hunting camp would be well advised to adopt a similar philosophy of operation.

As owner of the Pine Hill Club, I am very proud of our membership. To the person, they are truly a "circle of steel."

Off Season Activities – Pig Roast

We believe a family deer camp should be a year-round center of activity for the membership. The stalking and harvesting of deer obviously highlight camp goals, but this is only one element of many that combine to make a great camp.

At the Pine Hill Club, the membership meet on a regular basis for planned activities that enhance the bonding and fellowship enjoyed by the hunters.

For example, during the summer months members and their families participate in an old-fashioned picnic at the camp. A local caterer prepares a roast pig and provides all the trimmings. Beans, sweet corn, potatoes and cabbage salad highlight the menu for the camp picnic. Cakes, cookies and homemade pies are placed on a large table and participants heap their plates with the goodies.

Families are encouraged to participate in this event. Games are provided for all ages. Water-balloon tosses, sack races, and horseshoes are always on the list of activities to engage both young and old alike. Members meet children, wives and girlfriends. Youngsters thrive in this beehive of family activities.

Prizes are awarded for contest winners. Excitement and laughter surround the camp from sunrise to sunset. Children play games like hide-and-seek and race playfully through the wooded area surrounding the cabin. Adults enjoy a euchre tournament and the shared pleasure of kindred souls.

A large tent is erected to provide shade and shelter from the elements. Numerous picnic tables are placed in a circle to allow the guests and camp members a place to enjoy the goodies of the day.

The deer camp at this time resembles a scene from days gone by as young and old alike share in good-natured family fun.

Wood-Cutting Day

In addition to the summer pig roast, the camp also holds scheduled work bees for the members.

For example, club participants annually gather in the spring for a wood-cutting day at the camp. With saws, trailers and splitter at the ready, members harvest winter blow-downs and surplus trees on the camp property. These logs are transported to the cabin, where they are cut and split into proper lengths for the fireplace.

Each year the camp woodshed is filled to overflowing with split poplar and oak for the fires to come in the fall hunting season. Our woodshed holds ten cords of firewood, virtually all of which is burned during the cold Michigan winter evenings that occur from October through March.

Work crews are formed and divided into categories, including cutters, haulers, splitters and stackers. All members have a job to do. Together, the task is made simple and within roughly four hours, the woodshed is filled. Following this task all members stand back and admire the results of their labor.

A special bonding occurs among members at such times. Many stories from past seasons are repeated and good-natured joking and laughter abound during these workdays. Members greet others with camp nicknames. New family additions are noted and congratulations are granted to those citing achievements.

Joe has a new promotion! Jamie is getting married! Bob is retiring! All are examples of information exchanged during wood-cutting day at the Pine Hill Club. This exchange of family news provides for additional bonding among members.

Doug McFarlane and Bob Franks feed wood splitter on camp wood-cutting day.

Pine Hill Club cabin after wood cutting day.

An ample supply of wood for the coming season is prepared, but the day provides more than just hard work for the membership. This special time allows members to reflect on their relationships with each other and the deer camp. It helps create a positive atmosphere and builds anticipation for the upcoming season and the challenges of hunting the whitetail buck.

Processing Meat

Any successful deer camp provides an abundant supply of venison. With deer hanging on the buck pole, the challenge of processing meat becomes a group effort at the Pine Hill Club.

The camp owns, thanks to member donations, a meat grinder, freezer and ample space in the cabin for processing the game. Members eagerly share in the task of skinning, boning and slicing the delicious meat into the proper cuts for future meals.

Usually by the third or fourth day of season, the hunters will schedule a processing day for the venison harvested earlier. The chore of butchering the meat is shared by all, and work crews are divided into skinners, cutters, grinders and wrappers.

Meat is individually processed for the successful hunters, with appropriate names attached to each package. Each hunter selects how he wants his meat processed and individual sacks of processed meat are placed in the large freezer housed on the property.

The afternoon is filled with laughter and friendly joking about the deer shot. Successful hunters often describe in detail their personal achievements.

As with all hunting tales, the stories always get better with time and the shots prove more enjoyable and difficult after each colorful rendition. This day is always a special one of enjoyment and bonding, which is combined with the satisfaction of a full freezer of well-processed meat.

The meat-cutting day is a tradition at the Pine Hill Club and has been a part of the camp ritual since the very beginning.

Visitors at the Camp

Successful deer camps are a haven for visiting hunters from neighboring camps. The Pine Hill Club is frequented throughout the season by fellow hunters and other visitors who drop by, curious to "See how you did."

Evenings, after sundown, a steady flow of visitors arrives at our camp. Neighbors admire the deer harvested and successful hunters repeat their stories. Some visitors bring their bucks to camp for viewing. An atmosphere of happiness and success abounds as hunters exchange stories about individual success or failure during the day's hunt.

Regular camp visitors freely join in camp euchre games and oftentimes bring gifts to the camp. A bottle of homemade wine, some potatoes for the cook, or mementos collected during the summer are among items shared with the happy hunters.

The atmosphere is always joyous! Bucks are on the pole and the size of racks are reviewed and admired by those from the area, the campfire burns brightly, and good fellowship abounds.

"How did you do?" is the most frequently asked question.

"Who got the big eight-pointer?" asks another.

"What a beautiful deer!" is also a common exclamation as bucks on the pole are admired.

Only the deer hunter knows this atmosphere of camaraderie sitting by the fireplace and exchanging stories. It is exactly the type of goal we wished to attain when Al and I made our fateful decision to open the Pine Hill Club opportunities to other hunters.

A deer camp is truly an American tradition!

Camp Life Pranks

Deer camps maintain a special place in American society. Often included among their traditions is a very special and unique brand of humor. Laughing, joking, kidding, and card playing are obviously deeply ingrained in most deer camps.

The Pine Hill Club is no exception! Hunters enjoy joking with one another and good-natured pranks head their list of special memories.

As in most deer camps, members have a nickname, usually based on some personal attribute, physical characteristic or particular hunting style. Nicknames, once assigned, remain throughout the time of membership. The Pine Hill Club has a long tradition of nicknames for most members, including:

Bobcat	Bob Mills
Bucky	Bert Palmer
Red Nose	Kirk Coston
Quido Sarduchy	Ron Williams
Honest Jim	Jim Ward, Sr.
Big Jim	Jim Ward, Jr.
Gibber	Geoff Quick
Panama Jack	Roger Dixon
Trigger	Todd Walter
Pappa Joe	Joe Reihl
Coach	Chick Sherwood
Rocky	Terry Oswald
Bear	John Tyler
Smokey	Dick Tyler
Snake	Wayne Coston
Buckrub	Al Quick
Brewster	Bruce Anderson
Killer	Dave Mills
Sarge	Tom Peters
Carpy	Jim Collins

Ricky . . . . .Patrick Mills
Mac . . . . .Doug McFarlane
Geraldine . . . ."Our Beloved Outhouse"

Some members have not yet been dubbed with a nickname. Nicknames emerge and over time everyone will get a handle. It may take years, however, before someone earns a deer camp name, but sooner or later a particular event, characteristic or happening will identify a person. When this occurs, they will be christened and the name will stick with them for the remainder of their years in the deer camp.

Traditions such as this one, however minor, are a big part of deer hunting.

Pranks are also an integral ingredient of a deer camp. They certainly occur with some frequency at the Pine Hill Club. For instance:

Girly Pictures for a Hunting Blind

When John Tyler and Bruce Anderson papered Dick Tyler's hunting blind with pictures from a "girly" magazine, this event generated many laughs and remains to this day a topic of good-natured kidding. Dick Tyler was 78 years old when this decorating occurred and he still likes to tell about his reaction to the posting of pictures in his hunting stand.

"When it started to get light, I was somewhat shocked and certainly surprised at the unusual collage of pictures," Dick said. He reminisces with a smile about not being able to watch for deer because of the distraction from all the photographs.

Members still joke with him about not getting his deer that year because of his pre-occupation with the pictures. Dick just laughs, grins and takes the ribbing in good stride.

Orange Tennis Shoes

Spray painting camp cook Tom Peters' tennis shoes orange was another trick that still provides many chuckles at the deer camp.

One warm, sunny day, while Tom was sound asleep on the top of a camp picnic table, with his feet hanging over the end (Tom is 6' 4" tall) one of the hunters took a can of fluorescent orange paint and sprayed Tom's tennis shoes.

When Tom awoke, he rubbed his eyes and began to walk around camp before finally noticing his rather unique footwear.

"Who in the hell painted my shoes?" he bellowed!

Everyone laughed and pleaded innocent to this prank. Many hours of good-natured kidding followed, as Tom walked around the rest of the day in the brightly colored tennis shoes.

Pictures of the event adorn the walls to this day!

The Giant Bow Quiver

Dave Mills has a history of shooting many arrows at deer. He likes to shoot! As a result of this propensity, several members built a large bow quiver from 12" PVC pipe and labeled it with large black letters — "DAVE'S QUIVER."

They added about 25 old, broken arrows in this giant canister and then left it on the table for Dave to find the next morning, just prior to the opening day of bow season.

Dave saw it and laughed. "Who did this?" he asked.

As usual, no one admitted guilt. All gave the names of other persons.

"I didn't do it," said Ron. "It must have been Roger."

Roger immediately responded, "I didn't do it. Probably it was Joe," and so on around the camp table.

Dave expressed his sincere appreciation to all the members for the "present," before departing on his morning hunt. (As a point of interest, with not a little irony, he picked up a nice buck that day.)

This quiver still adorns the living room of the cabin and is a conversation piece for visitors, as well as a regular topic of humor among the members.

Fluffy

When member Wayne Coston shot a large coyote and hung the 65-pound male on the buck pole, he received much good-natured ribbing.

Joe Mills has a Siberian Husky dog that looks very much like a coyote. Joe claimed Wayne had shot his dog. "You shot Fluffy," laughed Joe.

Camp members roared as Wayne stoically denied shooting Joe's dog.

The next morning Joe tied a large pink ribbon around the coyote's neck with the name "Fluffy" written in large black letters. Wayne later had the hide tanned. It hangs now in the Pine Hill Club cabin, with the pink ribbon reattached to the neck of the cured hide.

Camp members still chuckle about Wayne shooting "Fluffy," now a permanent fixture at the Pine Hill Club cabin.

The Decoy Buck

New camp members are often the targets of good-natured pranks. This frequently is part of the ritual of becoming a new member in any hunting camp, much less at the Pine Hill Club.

When Terry Oswald, a retired gas station owner and oil product salesman, joined the camp several years ago, we reminded him that he must shoot only six-point bucks.

"Don't shoot a buck with less than six points. Be sure to count the points," we told him.

The night before the opening day of season, several members placed a six-point buck decoy about 50 yards from Terry's hunting stand. They placed the decoy in a narrow shooting lane to the left of his primary window.

When early morning daylight arrived, Terry saw the buck slowly emerge from the fog and darkness. He watched it in his scope. It didn't move as Terry adjusted his magnification from low to high, before finally realizing it was a decoy.

Of course everyone in the camp, except Terry, knew about the deer and could hardly wait until they returned that evening to learn of Terry's reaction.

Terry, however, did not mention anything about the buck decoy when he returned. Finally, Joe asked, "Terry, how do you gut out a styro-foam deer?"

Everyone laughed as Terry grinned and smiled about the event, "Who put the decoy in my shooting lane?"

Obviously, no one admitted guilt, but all roared with laughter.

The ability to take good-natured kidding in a deer camp is critical for the success of the overall camp. Members who pout, get angry, or want to argue can only cause dissention.

Camp members should be very carefully chosen, as one bad apple could truly spoil the hunting environment for all camp members.

Lunch Sack Prank

Another camp prank occurred when the members were packing lunches recently for the opening day of hunting season. (At the Pine Hill Club, we use an assembly line the night before for packing opening day lunches for the 21 members.)

Four or five members pack lunches for the entire group. Two sandwiches, an apple, candy bars and cookies are the norm. Each member prepares his or her own thermos of coffee, hot chocolate or soda.

Lunch sacks are labeled with the names of the individual hunters and are stored in a large cooler on the porch of the cabin for the next day's hunt.

One season, the packers decided to play a joke on Al Quick. They put cardboard between the slices of meat in his sandwiches and left the rest of his lunch the same as the others.

Al suspected nothing as he grabbed his lunch for the day's hunt.

That evening, everyone in the camp waited for Al's reaction to his cardboard lunch. Lighthearted kidding and much laughter erupted, when Al pointedly informed his colleagues that he "didn't appreciate" his special lunch.

All, of course, denied any knowledge of the altered sandwiches.

Recording the Snoring

When Kirk Coston, a computer programmer from Chicago, arrived at the breakfast table opening morning several members chided him about his snoring.

"I don't snore," retorted Kirk.

"Yes, you do," chimed in John and Bruce.

"You snore like a chain-saw," replied several other members, who had occupied the same bunkroom.

"You rattled the timbers," quipped Joe. "I couldn't sleep through all that commotion!"

The following night, one member produced a small tape-recorder and made a tape of Kirk's snoring.

The next morning at breakfast, the member shared at high volume proof of Kirk's snoring.

"Listen to this," he said, pressing the play button.

Raucous sounds of snoring roared throughout the lodge amidst the laughter of all, including Kirk.

"What can I say," he responded. "I really don't think that was me, but I did sleep very well…obviously unlike some of you."

Clearly, being somewhat thick skinned is a necessary attribute in any deer camp. Jokes and kidding are simply and irrefutable part of the ritual.

Learning to laugh together and at yourself, not taking life too seriously, are mandatory elements in the bonding of the membership.

Managing the Resources For Future Generations

In a more serious light, quality deer camps throughout the nation are concerned about managing their resources for future generations. These resources of woods, game, water and land all contribute to the preservation and continuation of quality hunting. All serious hunters are in agreement that they must be shepherds, caring for these natural resources and nurturing them to provide for good hunting for the generations to come.

Additionally, the resource of young, future hunters is a critical — if not the single most critical — resource for the continued, improved future of hunting.

At the Pine Hill Club, a series of resource management practices take place on an annual basis. Our camp has always worked closely with the Michigan Soil Conservation Service and the Michigan Department of Natural Resources to expand and improve habitat for game through proven conservation practices.

Over the past 30 years, we have planted over 150,000 red pine, Scotch pine, autumn olive, oak, walnut and Austrian pine trees on camp property. These plantings provide ground cover, shelter and food for the numerous deer, turkeys, partridge, squirrels and rabbits that inhabit the land. The trees prevent soil erosion and water run-off. The cover also provides nesting places for rabbits and coyotes, as well as the other indigenous wildlife.

In addition to planting trees, the camp has annually engaged in food plot management. Each year whitetail clover, rye grasses and buckwheat are planted to maintain a quality source of nutrients for the game. These crops are planted in conjunction with guidelines from the Michigan

Farm Service Agency and are based on conservation practices recommended to provide optimum food and shelter for wildlife.

Selective cutting of aspen and maple trees is another practice utilized at the Pine Hill Club to improve the natural habitat for deer and other game animals. The young shoots and heavy foliage resulting from this form of woodland management practice provide added cover and food for the game.

A trained forester has designed a constantly reviewed and updated wildlife management plan for the Pine Hill Club. This plan allows for knowledgeable future decision-making regarding the best management practices for the property and serves as a blueprint for future action.

In addition to adding food plots, selective cutting and tree planting, the club also has planted fruit trees at scattered locations for the game animals. Apple trees enhance the land and provide succulent fruit for many varieties of wildlife.

Management of the resources to provide quality hunting and game habitat for future generations is a major responsibility for any deer camp. Dense cover allows for bedding areas for the game and also enhances the habitat and environment. Some of the red pine trees we planted in 1972 are now over 30 feet tall. They provide windbreaks and food plots for birds, as well as cover for deer and other game.

Turkeys and partridge abound in the area of new plantings, feed off the new shoots and find shelter from predators in the dense foliage of the pine and aspen thickets.

Plantings, food plots and selective cuttings improve the protection of the natural resource. These practices will maintain the land for future generations as well as providing new growth and shelter for the game. As noted, successful, responsible deer camps always maintain the habitat properly for future hunters. The Pine Hill Club is no exception!

Perhaps the greatest single resource we work with in managing for the future at the Pine Hill Club is the ever-present group of young, future hunters who fall under our tutelage.

As noted earlier, Al and I first purchased the initial property in an attempt to provide a safe hunting environment for ourselves and our families. This goal quickly grew to encompass a desire to help our sons grow into successful deer hunters, as well as quality human beings, through our influence and the influence of other role models in their world.

Mentoring of young hunters has become perhaps the greatest single effort of the Pine Hill Club membership as we work to manage the resources for future generations. The generations are truly the most critical single resource for all of us.

It is for these future generations that Al and I expanded the membership of the Pine Hill Club beyond our immediate families. It is for these future generation members that we exist, and it is through sharing our knowledge and experiences with them that we take our greatest pleasure in this life.

Membership in the Pine Hill Club encompasses much more than just shooting deer! That's the simple part!

Young hunters — Cody Anderson, Jake Mills and Joe Mills take target practice. Note slingshot and BB guns.

CHAPTER 3

Opening Day at Deer Camp

Opening day of deer season is the super bowl of hunting! In Michigan nearly one million hunters take to the woods on opening day.

Throughout the average deer hunting season in Michigan, approximately 500,000 animals are harvested with bow, rifle and muzzleloader. Most are taken on the opening day of rifle season.

This event closes schools, makes wives temporary widows, and fills sporting goods stores with hunters seeking the latest in equipment and supplies for the hunt. Enthusiasts, both old and young, carefully count the days to the opening of deer season. The atmosphere is one of festivity, excitement, anticipation and full-throttle activity.

Opening morning of deer season is a most special time at the Pine Hill Club. Hearts pound a little faster and dreams of trophies dance in the heads of both veteran and novice hunters. Inarguably, it is Christmas Day for deer hunters!

As noted, half of all the bucks taken in Michigan's firearm season are shot on opening day. Therefore, opening day has very special meaning to all deer hunters.

With lunches packed, blinds ready and guns sighted in, hunters anxiously await the first early light of dawn.

At the Pine Hill Club, our camp alarm is set for 4:00 a.m. Hunters know the importance of being ready and prepared and all get up very early. The alarm bell signals the beginning of another opportunity to challenge the trophy whitetails.

Wayne Coston, a local plumber, and Jim Ward, Sr., a retired superintendent of schools, and I usually get up early and start the coffee, stoke the fireplace and get the table ready for the hungry hunters. This activity, combined with the alluring smell of frying bacon, awakens many members. Jim likes to tell jokes to one and all and Wayne has a loud, raucous laugh. The three of us scurry around the kitchen in anticipation of sleepy hunters, ready to eat.

Breakfast is always huge at our camp on opening morning. Pounds of bacon, dozens of eggs, loaves of toasted bread, and stacks of fresh pancakes highlight our arsenal of food. Three large coffee makers are used to brew coffee both for breakfast and to fill thermos bottles for the blinds. Orange, apple and tomato juice are also served.

Hunters start appearing about 4:30 a.m. A wake-up bell rings at 5:00 a.m. to roust the final sleepers. (The camp has a large bell that rings to signal meals.)

Breakfast is ready by 5:15 a.m. Hunters rub sleepy eyes and talk about the big buck they are going to shoot. Amid the laughter and pre-hunt excitement, a $2 buck pool is collected from each hunter for the first buck shot (honor system) and the biggest buck taken for the entire season.

The biggest buck includes bow, rifle and muzzle-loading season and is awarded to the lucky hunter at the end of the hunting period. The first buck shot by a successful rifle hunter is paid on opening night, with lots of good-natured kidding about time of day the trophy was harvested.

Never have we had a question about who shot the first buck, as members shooting a buck near the same time will decide, between themselves, which was the first buck killed.

Annually, the name of the big buck winner is placed on a plaque and displayed on the cabin wall. A listing of Pine Hill Club big buck winners by year is found in the appendix.

Following opening-day breakfast, hunters relax with a final cup of coffee and get ready to suit-up for the hunt. Excitement is always high as hunters look for their flashlight or gun case. The camp is a huge pile of orange coats, suspenders, thermos bottles, and rifles, racked and ready for the woods.

Despite the addition of indoor plumbing, Geraldine is usually called into action on opening morning at the Pine Hill Club. Good-natured joking and best wishes are exchanged, as members scurry to the woods and their favorite blind.

Members start to leave the camp no later than 6:00 a.m. All

Members gather in front of cabin prior to opening day of rifle deer season.

members will be in the woods by 6:30 a.m. at the very latest. All are poised for success with dreams of a trophy buck running through their heads.

The first day of season at the Pine Hill Club is an all-day affair. Members do not return to the cabin until dark. No one walks around the woods during the day. Movement is limited to members going to and from their individual hunting stands. Each hunter has a blind with a stove, chair, windows and a carpeted floor. There, he will remain from dawn till dark.

Hunting is obviously conducted in comfort in the blind. The long day is filled with waiting, watching and trying to stay alert for a trophy whitetail buck. Many hunters have a cache of supplies stored in their hunting blind, including candy and magazines, to supplement the sandwiches packed the night before.

The serene, noisy silence of the woods is usually broken about 7:00 a.m., as the first shots ring out, signaling the beginning of another season. The opening blasts echo throughout the woods and thoughts of another hunter putting venison on the pole and tagging the first buck of the camp spin through every member's head.

At the Pine Hill Club, each member knows where the others hunt. Early shots reflect the potential success of the member in specified locations.

"Joe got his buck!"… "Geoff shot a deer!" Members know.

A shot in the immediate hunting area also puts any stand hunter on full alert. The sound not only signals deer are moving, it is possible the shooter missed. A trophy buck may bolt through an open trail or sneak down a nearby runway.

Excitement mounts as other shots are fired. Hunters celebrate or curse, depending on the success of their shot. What an exciting event!

As time passes and more deer are sighted, hunters begin a mental record of the number of does, fawns and smaller bucks observed at their assigned stand. (Note: Pine Hill Club hunters shoot only six point or larger bucks and only mature does.)

A Personal Opening Day Perspective

Eagerly settling into my stand I anticipate seeing deer at any moment. I watch intently, keeping check on the same runways time and time again.

All of the sudden, I see movement. Slowly bringing up my binoculars and getting them to full focus, I spot a plump fox squirrel feeding and storing acorns in preparation for the short winter days due in December. Shucks! No deer yet! It is 10:00 a.m.

"Where are they?" I ask myself.

Another shot breaks the silence to the west. "Wayne Coston got his buck," I think, "or maybe it is Geoff Quick."

It is difficult to tell the direction of a single shot from over a mile away. Another movement catches my eye and I am again on full alert.

As I peer carefully into the dense woods, a doe slowly appears. With this deer are two other smaller deer, probably her fawns of the previous spring. Another doe appears and then another. They all move cautiously down the runway I am watching.

They stop to feed occasionally and are on full alert, as they carefully continue along the pathway.

Suddenly, a doe jerks her head up and stares behind her, as if expecting a visitor.

With ears wide-open, the deer stands like a cement statue. The other deer also come to full alert and stand motionless, much like soldiers at attention.

I note a slight movement in the direction the deer are looking. A body slowly emerges with its head down, as if smelling the ground. After what seems like an eternity, this deer finally lifts its head, revealing a well-polished rack of golden yellow antlers.

The buck stands, looks, smells the air and proceeds with caution. He constantly surveys the immediate area and listens for sounds of danger.

I slowly count the points in my scope – 5,6,7,8. Deciding that I am going to shoot the deer when he turns broadside, I continue to remain motionless and quiet.

Holding my rifle, I steady the cross hairs of my scope on the buck's shoulders, take careful aim and slowly squeeze the trigger.

The .270 roars and the 130-grain Nosler partition bullet finds its mark. The buck drops like a ton of bricks.

I quickly chamber another shell and watch the buck for signs of life. He is down! After five minutes, I flip the safety on, pull on my boots and prepare to exit my stand.

(Note: When I sit in my stand, I remove my boots and keep my stocking feet on the floor. The carpet is soft and this procedure allows me to shift my feet with minimum noise. This is a practice I have used for years).

Proceeding slowly toward the downed buck, I admire the beautiful animal from a distance. My heart hammers as a unique adrenaline rush flows throughout my body. No street drug could produce such a thrill! I believe there is no more challenging trophy than a mature, woods-smart, whitetail buck. Harvesting one is an achievement that never pales.

I quickly note the deer is dead. Propping the rifle in a safe place and looking again at the beautiful buck, I am awed with this magnificent trophy.

As I prepare for the field dressing process, I shake with excitement. No matter how many bucks I shoot, the feeling of accomplishment and wonder is always the same.

Tagging the deer, rolling my sleeves up, taking off my watch and readying my Marble knife for the familiar chore, I roll the buck over and quickly finish the field dressing process.

This process has been performed hundreds of times over my nearly 50 years of hunting the whitetail. Field dressing is a simple chore to a veteran hunter.

Propping the buck open to allow the carcass to cool and drain, I again admire this beautiful animal.

"Wow", I think, "What an adrenaline rush!"

As I clean my hands in the snow, I return to my blind to wash my hands with the jug of water stored for that very purpose. Drying my hands on a paper towel left in the blind, I sit down, take off my boots and pour another cup of hot coffee.

Checking my watch, I note it is now 10:30 a.m. With my buck secured, I now have approximately seven hours left to enjoy the woods and the joy of hunting the most challenging animal in the forest.

The pressure is off! I know I can hang the trophy on the buck pole after dark. I also know my colleagues will congratulate me and admire this beautiful eight-point buck.

Back at the Camp

"How wide is the spread?"

"How much does it weight?"

"What time did you shoot it?"

"Did it run?"

All are common questions hunters ask about each buck on the pole.

"He is a beauty. Congratulations! Way to go!" shouts still another member.

There is nothing like a deer camp for a hunter who shoots a buck.

On opening night, the camp is a beehive of activity as the hunters return with their kills.

As the hunters slowly arrive at camp, the day's stories are repeated many times. Ten bucks hang on the pole. One buck with a tight basket rack of six points adjoins another with a wide-beamed rack of ten points.

"What time did you shoot your deer?" is frequently asked as successful Pine Hill Club members begin to think about collecting half of the buck pool for the first buck taken on opening day. Good-natured kidding always takes place, as members relate the time they shot their deer.

The laughter continues as the hunters complete dinner and

settle sleepily before the roaring fire burning in the huge stone fireplace.

Hunters compare notes on deer seen, coyotes sighted and other information regarding their opening day in the woods.

One responds about a mouse in his stove, another tells of a large porcupine

Rifles ready for opening day.

climbing the tree next to his stand, and a third reports a buck herding does like a rodeo pony herds cows.

Joking and laughter continue as neighbors arrive from area camps. All share stories and enter into the celebration that can only be appreciated by hunters hanging a buck on opening day.

Some hunters prepare for early bed, while others circle a large campfire in an attempt to continue the magic of the day. Still others engage in a game of euchre. Excitement fills the air and the fire burns brightly for those who have filled their tag and those who dream of doing so.

"Wow," I think, "there is nothing like opening day in a deer camp!"

Reflecting on the day's events, I pull the goose-down sleeping bag over my head and prepare for a night of much needed rest. I revisit the buck walking down the runway and replay the day's hunt as I drift into a dream-filled sleep.

CHAPTER 4

Four Sons & Their First Bucks

ew memories are more precious to a father than those created through sharing in his son's first successful deer hunt. As noted earlier, having a safe environment to hunt with my sons and sharing such moments were among the prime motivations for purchasing the Pine Hill Club property.

My wife, Marge, and I have four sons: Mike, Dave, Joe and Rick. The boys are approximately one year apart in age. All grew up enmeshed in the tradition of deer hunting.

The Pine Hill Club has provided everyone associated with it a safe, quality deer-hunting environment with wonderful family memories for nearly 30 years. In this light, I would be remiss as a father and as a raconteur if I did not share a brief description of each of my sons' first buck taken there.

To this day, these fine young men still actively pursue the joy and challenge of stalking whitetail deer, although never as intently as during their impossible-to-duplicate, unforgettable first hunts.

Mills boys — Author with four sons, Mike, Dave, Joe, Rick.

Mike's First Buck

When our son Mike was born on January 30, 1961, my wife, Marge, and I were elated! We celebrated the birth of this, our first child, with many delightful hours of discussion about his possible future and the potential hunter we had added to our family.

Marge is not a hunter, but she is very supportive of our deer hunting interests. She has shared with me, on many occasions, the unique joy of the Michigan woods. She loves the outdoors and often visits the open spaces and wood lots at the Pine Hill Club with me.

Like many other Pine Hill Club spouses, she enjoys cross-country skiing, mushroom hunting and berry picking at the deer camp during the off season.

I bought Mike his first shotgun at age five. It was an Ithaca, single shot, 20 gauge. Between my .22 rifle and the 20 gauge, he became proficient at shooting targets and cans, while he waited, eagerly, until he was

12 to be able to purchase his first small game hunting license. When Mike began hunting, he killed his first rabbit and squirrel on the Pine Hill Club property.

We shared many long walks in the woods as he learned gun safety and respect for the game we sought in the forest.

At age 14, Mike was ready for deer camp. Having spent several years sitting with me in my stand, he was ready to begin his solo experience at hunting the elusive whitetail.

Together, we built a stand at a point of land where an oak-covered ridge adjoined a cedar swamp. Numerous runways criss-crossed the point and it was a natural funnel for whitetails seeking to utilize the thick cover of the cedars.

Mike carried his grandfather's .308 Winchester M-l00. An extra clip of ammo was in his pocket and a new Case hunting knife, with a leather handle, hung from his belt. (Note: He stills carries this original Case knife today!)

Clothed in warm boots and the traditional Michigan deer hunter red Soo Wool pants and coat, he was ready for the long- awaited challenge of deer hunting.

At 7:30 a.m. on opening day, Mike first saw motion behind a large oak tree, only 30 feet from his stand. His first deer of his first season appeared!

The deer slowly emerged into full view. At such a close distance, Mike could see the beautiful rack on the sleek, fat, whitetail. He excitedly counted at least eight points on the buck's rack.

Slowly raising his borrowed rifle, he took careful aim through the open sights and prepared to shoot. He gently pulled the trigger. Nothing happened!

Mike checked the safety. It was off. He pulled again and again, nothing!

The deer whirled, raised its white flag and bounded into the safety of the cedar swamp. What a disappointment it was for the young hunter!

An empty, lonely feeling filled his body. He had blown the shot of his dreams!

Checking his rifle, he discovered the bolt had not been fully closed. He slammed the bolt forward and sighed a disappointing breath, feeling like the only hunter who has ever missed a deer.

As I shared with Mike later that evening, I have never known of any veteran deer hunter who couldn't relate one or more similar stories about "blowing" an easy chance to kill a nice buck.

After several decades of deer hunting, I believe if you haven't missed a deer before, you probably haven't spent much time in the woods. Call it fate, buck fever, bad luck or human error, whatever — in time, every deer hunter will miss a deer and experience that empty feeling in their stomach. This only adds to making the challenge of hunting the elusive whitetail so exciting to young and old alike.

I shared Mike's disappointment! I really wanted him to shoot a buck.

Mike had seen 15 to 20 deer that day, but no other bucks presented a shot.

Earlier on opening morning, I had shot a wide-racked, four-pointer. When Mike and I arrived at camp, we found that Dick Kolaja, my brother-in-law, had also taken a huge 12-pointer. As noted in Chapter 1, this buck is still the camp record. Additionally, Chuck Pisoni had shot a symmetrical eight-pointer, only 100 yards behind the cabin. Our shared success only served to deepen Mike's disappointment and increase his resolve to harvest a buck of his own.

After a hot evening meal, we stoked the fire and prepared for an early bedtime. The long day in the woods had seemed like an eternity for the young hunter. I suggested to Mike that he take my trusty .30-.30 Winchester M-94 for his second day of hunting.

"All you have to do is pull the hammer back and shoot," I told Mike.

The next morning, with my Winchester in his hand and his supplies packed for the all-day hunt, I dropped Mike off at 6:10 a.m. for the short walk to his deer stand. He left my truck with a renewed commitment to get a deer.

Daylight arrived with a beautiful sunrise at approximately 7:00 a.m.

The woods were still, pristine and aglow with the early rays of a bright red sunrise sparkling off crystal snow. I poured a cup of coffee and settled back for a long wait.

A single shot rang out from Mike's direction at 9:00 a.m. I immediately knew it was Mike shooting. No more shots followed. I waited for what seemed like an eternity, but what in reality was only three or four minutes.

"Tweet-Tweet," went Mike's whistle.

Shaking with excitement, I exited the blind, knowing my first born son had shot at his first buck. It was hard for me to contain my excitement as I proceeded through the cattails toward the oak point, where Mike was located.

When I got within 50 yards from his stand, I saw Mike standing in a clump of cedars. Hardly able to contain my anxiety, I shouted, "Did you get a deer?".

"Yes," he responded.

"Is it a buck?" I asked, thinking he might have shot a doe following his excitement after missing the buck the day before, because his gun didn't fire.

"Yes, I shot a buck!" Mike responded.

I increased my pace and quickly closed the distance between myself and the point where Mike stood admiring his first deer. The buck was a beautiful, large-bodied spike-horn.

Mike was extremely proud and excited about shooting his first deer, but no more so than I.

I contend there is no single greater thrill in hunting than sharing such a wonderful and special moment with your child. It is a memory that will last each of you a lifetime. Hunters always remember their first buck. So do their fathers, especially if the father is fortunate enough to be present at this life-altering moment.

"Dad, the deer came walking from the north and was behind me," exclaimed Mike. "I saw spikes and waited until he came into full view and was broadside before I shot.

"He dropped immediately, not knowing what hit him. I racked another shell in the gun and waited, but he was down for good. That's when I blew the whistle for you."

The rest is history!

Together, we field dressed the deer and dragged it to a large oak tree. There with a short piece of rope, we hoisted it about one foot off the ground to let it hang to properly drain. We propped open the chest cavity and decided to return to the camp, as we now both had shot a deer.

In camp we repeated the story over and over, exchanging hugs and pats on the back. Mike had shot his first whitetail buck!

Later in the day we returned to drag the buck to my truck and proudly hang the deer on the buck-pole. We now had four bucks on our camp buck-pole. Mike's buck, although not the largest deer, was particularly special because it was his first deer.

Following dinner, we drove to town so Mike could call his mother and announce the success of his first hunt. Mike had many stories and memories to share with his classmates at school. He now had proven himself a successful deer hunter!

Dave's First Buck

Our second son Dave was three years old when I carried him on my shoulders into the deer woods on a sunny Friday after Thanksgiving. He was bundled in warm clothes with a red snowsuit providing warmth. He wanted to go with me deer hunting and I decided I would take him out in the afternoon for about an hour of quiet time in the woods.

Dave was a typical three-year old. He liked to ask questions and wanted to explore everything. He loved to go camping and watch the bonfire. His love of the out-of-doors was very apparent on our family camping trips to northern Michigan.

Even though over 30 years have passed, I still remember this day vividly. The weather was clear, temperatures were in the high 20's and a skiff of snow was on the ground. The woods were beautiful as we walked a quarter mile to the birch-covered edge of a cedar swamp.

We were hunting private property in Gladwin County. Our entire family was visiting at my parents' home in northern Gladwin County, well-known prime deer country.

As I placed Dave beside me, near a large pine stump, I cuddled against him and relaxed my back against the solid stump. My trusty .30-.30 Winchester M-94 lay within arm's reach should a buck appear. Within minutes, Dave was sound asleep.

About 20 minutes passed as I enjoyed the serenity of this beautiful, peaceful setting. I thought to myself, "How can life get much better?"

All of the sudden, seemingly out of nowhere, four deer appeared. One was a fork-horn buck. The deer were totally unaware of our presence.

I slowly raised my rifle, took careful aim at the buck and fired. The buck dropped immediately.

Dave raised his head and asked, sleepily, "What happened?"

"I shot a deer," I replied.

Gathering Dave in my arms, we walked to the downed buck. Celebrating as best I could with a three-year-old, I sat Dave on the ground, secured my rifle at a safe distance, and proceeded to tag the buck and field dress the animal.

I hiked back with Dave triumphantly perched on my shoulders. I savored the events that had occurred within the past hour. I shall never forget this unique hunt with my young son Dave, nor shall he.

Once David was old enough to deer hunt, he also had proven himself proficient with both a .22 rifle and a shotgun. I was anxious for him to challenge the mighty whitetail.

With proper clothing, my trusty .30-.30 Winchester M-94 and full compliment of sandwiches and other goodies, Dave took his stand on an aspen-covered ridge overlooking a heavily traveled runway near a cattail swamp on Pine Hill Club property.

As I sat in my nearby blind, I was alert for any sounds that might originate from the direction of Dave's stand. I knew he would be carefully monitored by his Uncle Vern, who was hunting nearby, and was in a warm, safe location to begin his virgin venture as a new deer hunter. That certainly didn't make me any less alert, however.

At 8:30 a.m., I heard a rifle shot from Dave's direction. I listened intently for more shots. Within one or two minutes, I heard four more shots in rapid succession! I listened for a whistle or other signal from Dave's direction. Nothing, only silence. I was certain Dave had fired the Winchester! No further sounds were forthcoming.

After 45 minutes, the suspense finally got to me. I decided to check with Dave and his Uncle Vern.

As I walked the long quarter mile, I was hoping and praying that Dave had shot his first buck. I was consumed by the suspense of the moment.

When I approached Dave's stand, I saw Uncle Vern and Dave standing about 50 yards from the blind. They were looking at a beautiful five-point buck that Dave had shot. I immediately hugged Dave, congratulated him on his accomplishment and admired the healthy, large-bodied five-pointer.

"Why did you shoot five times?" I asked Dave, who told me that his first shot had downed the deer.

Dave explained that as he approached, the deer was kicking slightly. Remembering I had told him to shoot a downed deer in the neck to be sure it was dead, he proceeded to shoot the deer four more times in the neck.

Excitement, emotions and adrenaline flow are integral parts of the deer hunting experience!

Dave was justly proud of his buck and of becoming a successful deer hunter. Needless to say, his father and uncle were equally proud of Dave's success.

Dave will always remember this hunt. It was 11:30 a.m. by the time we hung his trophy at camp. All was well at the Pine Hill Club and Dave spent the rest of the day celebrating his success and relaxing before the warm fire. It was a great day for a 14-year-old hunter ... and his Dad!

Over the years Dave has repeated the feat of bagging a whitetail buck many times.

Several large, wide-racked bucks hang over our camp fireplace. Two of Dave's best bucks are among these trophies. Both are heavy-horned, wide-racked eight-pointers.

None, however, has generated the excitement of that first buck, shot hunting with his Dad and his Uncle Vern.

Joe's First Buck

When Joe (Jeffrey) Mills was born, November 2, 1963, I had no doubts he was destined to follow in the hunting footsteps his older brothers would make.

Having positive role models and belonging to a family that has a strong and active passion about hunting whitetail deer, Joe entered an environment that encouraged him to learn the finer points of deer hunting.

As the years went by, Joe demonstrated an exceptionally keen interest in the great out-of-doors. He loved to be in the woods with his brothers, pretending to be a deer hunter. Joe also liked to climb trees and would go to the top of large trees as a four-year-old. My wife and I, as concerned parents, would shudder when we would see Joe high in a tree, fearing he might fall. He, on the other hand, had no fear of heights.

Our third son is a southpaw like his great grandfather Harry Mills.

Being the first southpaw in our immediate family required a firearm that would accommodate a left-handed shooter. His first shotgun was an Ithaca .20 gauge M-37 pump, which featured bottom ejection. I had a local gunsmith switch the safety to accommodate a left-handed shooter.

As with the other boys, Joe quickly became a skilled marksman and an excellent rifle shot. Also like them, by age 14 he was ready and eager to take on the challenge of hunting a whitetail buck.

The fall of 1977 found Joe at the Pine Hill Club with his older brothers and approximately ten other club members.

The Pine Hill Club by this time had expanded to include 200 acres of hunting property.

A spirit of excitement permeated the camp as all welcomed Joe to the camp. As is normal with a new member, Joe received much good-natured kidding. Taking the jokes in good stride, he displayed an inner excitement that can only be felt by an aspiring deer hunter.

On opening morning, Joe was placed in the same hunting blind where his brother Dave had killed his first buck. This blind, located in the center of the original 80 acres of Pine Hill Club property, had been named Buckhorn, because it was the site of the biggest buck ever killed on the property.

It was here where two years earlier in 1975 Dick Kolaja had shot his 12-pointer.

The location had proven to be a super hunting spot and Joe was thrilled to be placed in this stand.

The stand, located on an oak-covered ridge, afforded relatively close shooting, roughly 100 yards maximum. It was a great blind for a beginning hunter.

Like his brothers, Joe carried a .30-.30 Winchester M-94 carbine on his first hunt. The rifle had open sights and could be operated by either a right or left-handed shooter. He also carried a pair of eight-power binoculars in his backpack.

I dropped him off at 6:15 a.m. to begin his first hunt. The young man was ready for the challenge of his first morning of solo deer hunting.

Uncle Vern, as with Joe's brothers, hunted nearby to assist, if needed.

As I left for my stand, approximately three-quarters of a mile from the oak ridge that was home to Joe, I couldn't help but again reflect on how quickly children grow up and mature into young adults.

My morning hunt was quickly successful as a tight-racked eight-pointer strolled into my shooting lane at 8:05 a.m. One shot from my

Uncle Vern Mills gets dressed on opening morning.

trusty .270 Remington 700 dropped this buck in his tracks. I field dressed the deer, propped it open, and returned to my stand.

Tagging a buck on opening morning normally takes the pressure off of any hunter. This was not the case now, however, as I eagerly anticipated the excitement of Joe's hunt.

By 11:00 a.m., the suspense had gotten to me. Despite our "No walking around on opening day" rule, I had to check with Joe and see how he had done.

Arriving at the cabin, I met with Ron Williams, a police captain and longtime member of the camp. Ron had shot a nice buck at first light and had walked back to the cabin to relax and savor his success. He told me he believed Joe had shot at a deer.

I couldn't wait any longer. Gathering rope, knife, and orange tape in case we had to track Joe's deer, I started off to see how he had done.

Arriving at his stand, I observed Joe out of his blind, carefully searching the ferns surrounding his hunting stand.

"What did you shoot?" I asked.

Joe was visibly upset and trembled when he spoke....

"I shot a big spike-horn that was in velvet," he responded. "But, I can't find the deer," he said in frustration.

After explaining what happened, we both looked for blood or any other sign of a hit. Joe had finally found blood, but only small drops on the ferns. He said the deer had wheeled at his shot and headed for the wet swamp to the north.

Knowing that three hours had elapsed from the time Joe had first shot at the buck, I assured him that we would carefully track the whitetail.

The fact that he said he had shot a buck in velvet troubled me.

"Are you sure it was a buck?" I asked.

"I'm positive it was a buck, Dad. It had large horns, all in velvet," he repeated again. "I know it had horns and I know that I hit the deer. I just don't know where it is."

Moving slowly on the track, we inched along to the north toward the large wet swamp where the deer had fled. Joe had clearly hit the buck, as we located a few additional small flecks of blood. A lack of snow made the tracking very difficult.

I was determined to find Joe's first buck. Circling carefully each time I lost the trail of the wounded deer, Joe remained on the point of last blood. Time passed slowly as we patiently and carefully searched for the wounded animal.

Emerging from the swamp, the buck had continued north toward our fence-line. Blood sign was sparse, but with patience we covered approximately 300 yards from the point of the shot.

Searching carefully, I spotted a runway that lead into a brushy area. With Joe on the last blood, I proceeded cautiously into the brushy island. Finding more blood, I was confident the deer was close.

After searching about 30 yards into the brushy area, I suddenly spotted the deer on the ground ahead. It was still alive, but couldn't run. I approached the buck with caution and finished it off with one shot in the neck.

"Joe," I shouted, "Here is your buck!"

Joe was so excited about finding his deer he quickly picked his way through the brush and stood triumphantly over the downed whitetail.

The buck was not, as the excited young hunter had first thought, a spike-horn in velvet. It was a magnificent eight-pointer with a very symmetrical rack, 16 inches in width.

I thought of the small eight-pointer I had shot and knew immediately that this deer's rack was much bigger and wider.

By evening of that special opening day, club members had shot ten bucks. Five were eight-pointers. Joe's deer was the third largest. My eight-pointer was only fifth.

Joe's brother Dave was also successful, taking another beautiful eight-pointer with a wide rack and long golden yellow tines.

Dave eventually won the buck pool for the biggest buck taken that year, but Joe's buck, the largest ever taken as a Mills' son's first deer, was clearly the camp trophy for the season.

Rick's First Buck

Our youngest son Patrick (Rick) is two and one-half years younger than Joe. Being the last Mills' boy, he was also anxious to prove himself a worthy deer hunter, just like his brothers.

Rick wanted to hunt! He eagerly sought and listened to advice from the veteran hunters at camp and was often the brunt of good-natured kidding and joking as the youngest member in the camp.

Rick had the advantage of excellent role models who taught him scores of secrets about deer hunting. In addition to the many camp veterans, he had his three older brothers, who never hesitated to give him advice, direction and suggestions about what he should do to be successful.

Again, like his brothers, this young hunter became proficient with both rifle and a shotgun. He bagged many rabbits, squirrels and partridge on the property while learning to shoot and hunt.

Rick couldn't wait for the challenge of the mighty whitetail!

During the previous summer, before his 14th birthday, I bought Rick a .308 Remington 760, a pump rifle carbine with open sights. Rick practiced for hours with this rifle and became a very accurate shot with it.

He was our first son not to use the traditional .30-.30 Winchester M-94 to hunt his first buck.

Opening morning, 1980, found him up well before the light of dawn, eagerly rechecking his equipment and getting ready for his first day of hunting by himself for a whitetail buck. He carefully packed his gear in anticipation of his big day in the woods.

Rick was dressed in layers of wool, with warm boots and bright orange vest. He had an extra clip of shells. He was so anxious to take to the woods he could barely eat his breakfast.

Placing Rick in the same Buckhorn stand where Joe and Dave had killed their first bucks, I was confident that he would see many deer. Again, Uncle Vern was hunting close by and was available should Rick need assistance.

At 9:20 a.m., Rick spotted a large six-point buck walking along the runway, adjacent to the soggy swamp.

Carefully raising his rifle, he took steady aim and fired. The buck dropped immediately! The excited hunter pumped another shell in his rifle.

Watching the deer on the ground, Rick remained in his blind for about ten minutes.

Finally he proceeded, with caution, to the downed buck, checking to be certain it was dead.

Beaming with pride, he then walked to Uncle Vern's stand.

Rick field dressed the big buck as Uncle Vern coached him through the process.

After a day of anticipation on my stand, I eagerly returned to camp to learn of Rick's success.

Was I proud and happy? The excitement of his shooting a nice buck the first day of his first hunting season exceeded my most prayerful hopes!

Hours of practice had clearly paid off for Rick, who had shot his buck through the heart and shoulders, killing it immediately.

That night we all enjoyed liver and onions from Rick's deer. He was one proud hunter, but no prouder than his father.

Like all successful deer hunters, Rick retold the story many times. It got better with each repetition!

Deer hunting is truly an American tradition. Having four sons who all were successful in killing their first buck while hunting with me renewed and invigorated my faith in our deer camp. What marvelous invaluable memories!

As I grow older, I clearly remember with pride, love and satisfaction my four sons and their first bucks killed at the Pine Hill Club. Deer hunting memories last forever! These special ones will go with me to my grave!

Rick Mills with nice buck shot on fourth day of season.

CHAPTER 5

Camp Stories –"True Happenings"

*D*eer camps are shrouded with history and tradition. Most camps are notorious for the occurrence of comical and/or unusual events. The Pine Hill Club is no exception.

Daily humorous events take place within the smokey haunts of well-oiled rifles, bacon frying, card games and happy hunters surrounding a large glowing campfire.

The mystique and allure affiliated with such activities only add to the attraction of a deer camp. These shared experiences, more so than actually harvesting a nice buck, attract and enhance the members of the Pine Hill Club. These moments are special and memorable. Perhaps it is times such as these that entice such a diverse gathering of strong individuals to return each year to share their time with each other and to participate in this annual ritual.

Retold each season, the memories and stories truly get better with time. While the stories won't make the top ten television tales, they are very special to the members of our club family. We'd like to share a few of them with you.

Enjoy!

Uncle Vern's Lantern

Blowing his horn repeatedly, Uncle Vern arrived at the Pine Hill Club hunting camp two days before the opening of deer season. His grand entrance in the purple pickup he had painted by hand was always a welcome addition to the camp.

Uncle Vern was a gifted raconteur, who had the ability to motivate hunters with his numerous stories about former pursuits of the whitetail buck. He had been successful on many hunts, although his greatest stories weren't about his successes, but his failures. He shared many exciting stories of missing deer, of being outfoxed by the game, and truly doing dumb things while deer hunting. These tales were not about his most memorable trophies, they were invaluable instructions in the art of deer hunting.

As he recalled each story in vivid detail, he would wave his arms, raise his eyebrows, and laugh with gusto. His joy would spread throughout the camp and all would hold their sides chuckling, when he related stories about deer that had outsmarted him on previous hunts. We were always thrilled when he arrived. He was an inspiration and a mentor without peer.

As he emerged from the truck this year, we all exchanged the customary hugs, pats on the back and "Glad you're here!" greetings.

"Did you bring your gun?" I asked him in jest.

Uncle Vern grinned at the questions and proudly announced he had just installed a new sight on his trusty Winchester.

"Wait until you see it. This new sight just doesn't miss," he replied.

Pulling the old, battered Winchester lever action from the case, he proudly checked the chamber and handed it to me.

The sight was painted fluorescent orange. Uncle Vern displayed pride and satisfaction with this new addition to his rifle.

"What do you think?" he asked. "You'll be able to find this sight in the dark!"

"We'll let the buck pole do the talking," I responded.

"I bought a new lantern for my blind," he added proudly, pulling an ancient, battered, green lantern from the bed of his pickup.

"What do you think of this?"

"Does it work?" I quizzed.

"Does it work?" he responded. "Let me show you!"

The members gathered around Uncle Vern, more eager for his color-ful views than for the inauguration of his new lantern.

Most had some smart remark to share about both his lantern and truck.

"Did you paint your truck this year?" asked Dave.

"No! Don't you think it looks good?" he commented.

"You surely won't lose it in the snow," said Dave, amidst laughter at the good-natured exchange be-tween uncle and nephew.

"Watch this lantern work!" said Uncle Vern, as he attempted to light the old lantern with a match.

"Whuff!" went the lantern, as the gas ignited setting the entire unit in flames. As Uncle Vern attempted to quench the fire, we all roared in laughter.

"You are going to burn the woods down with that lantern," I said.

"Don't worry. At least I'll be warm," Uncle Vern grinned back.

Finally, getting the lantern under control, he stood back and admired his new prize.

Uncle Vern and Bob Caltrider cutting deer. Note Uncle Vern's grin.

"There. It just needed a little adjustment," he responded.

Again, we all laughed and made remarks about the Chicago fire, forest fires and burning the cabin to the ground with his new garage sale purchase.

While recalling this story I couldn't help but think about how mem-bers in a deer camp bond over time. Uncle Vern was an original hunter at the Pine Hill Club. He contributed joy, excitement and humorous stories about hunting to the members. His infectious grin, bushy eyebrows and animated story-telling kept all listeners on the edge of their seats. Uncle

Vern's sense of humor was always a pleasure to have in camp. He was easy going and a good camp cook, both invaluable qualities in a deer camp.

Uncle Vern took our good-natured kidding about his explosive lantern in stride, smiling and laughing. He was family to all who met him. Uncle Vern was a winner at the Pine Hill Club and in life.

All the members who were fortunate enough to know him were saddened by his death in 1991.

Bob's Fire Starter

Many deer camps have wood burning stoves, such as the one used at the Pine Hill Club. The early camp featured a vintage Warm Morning, firebrick-lined, wood stove, with a damper and eight-inch stovepipe that protruded through the ceiling of the original hunting shack. As the only source of heat, it was imperative to keep the fire going if hunters wished to stay warm.

Bob was self-appointed master of creative ways to start a fire in the old wood burner. His methods were often unique and sometimes dangerous. For example, he often would fire-up the old stove, using a mixture of his special "fire-starter."

"I'll get the stove going," Bob would proudly announce to the members.

"Don't blow yourself up," was the usual response.

Bob would laugh and proceed with his task of stoking the old wood burner.

His formula was a simple one: paper, dry wood kindling and his mixture of "fire-starter."

The stove had a 10-inch door on the top. Bob would peer into the mouth of the stove to see how it was going.

One memorable, frigid morning, members from the warm comfort of their sleeping bags urged Bob to get busy and get a fire going!

"I can see my breath," said Joe.

"The temperature must be 30 below. At least it feels like it."

"Get cracking!" directed Al.

Stoking the wood burner with paper and kindling, Bob proceeded to grab what he thought was a cup of his famous fire-starter. He poured the contents in the old stove and lighted a match.

"WOOSH!" went the fire, as it exploded in the sturdy stove. Flames roared out of the top of the stove, singeing Bob's eyebrows, beard and side-burns.

"Are you all right?" asked Tom.

"Are you sure you're OK?" quizzed Doug.

"I'm all right," replied Bob, brushing singed hair from his face. "I probably just put too much fire-starter in the stove."

"What did you use," quizzed Dave?

"I thought it was fuel oil. Instead, it was white-gas," said Bob. "Oops!"

Everyone laughed at the mistake, but all were relieved no real damage had occurred. Everyone knew the potential danger of his mixture.

"Mistake made! Lesson learned!" thought Bob.

The Florida Buck

Having just missed the biggest buck of my hunting career, I was reflecting on the complete effects of getting "buck fever" at the most inopportune moment. At 5:20 p.m., on opening day in 2000, a large 10-point buck had followed several does out of a heavily timbered swamp area near my blind.

I saw the does first and then noticed another deer following them through the heavy timber. Spotting an antler, I readied my rifle just in case a shootable six-point buck would appear.

Scoping the heavy timber, I spotted a large antlered buck standing near several other deer. He clearly exceeded the Pine Hill Club six-point minimum rack!

Not wanting to risk a poor shot, I waited until he walked into full-view and presented a better shot. Counting the points on the buck's antlers got my heart thumping. I knew the chance to harvest a lifetime record was near.

The buck stood, checked the wind, listened intently, and slowly moved one step at a time. Long periods of waiting were joined by an occasional movement on the runway toward where two does had appeared.

My heart was hammering! I didn't want to blow the shot. I waited... rifle ready for the buck to move into position. Finally, five long minutes later, after what seemed like an hour, the buck stepped out into a clearing.

Steadying my aim, I squeezed the trigger! BANG!

The large buck whirled and ran back into the heavy timber.

"Rats!" I said to myself. There was no chance for another shot.

I sat in disbelief that I had cleanly missed such a trophy. The other deer scattered at the sound of the .270 going off.

Putting on my boots, I tentatively, with trepidation and a sinking feeling in my chest, made the long journey to where the buck had been standing when I shot.

Certain I had missed, due to the reaction of the buck, I felt empty, lonely and depressed. Only deer hunters who have shared this most disheartening of moments can truly understand the experience.

"How could I have missed this deer?" I thought to myself. "I blew the chance of a lifetime!"

Circling the area, I found no sign of a hit in the snow. I was even more depressed. I knew deep down I had not connected with this trophy.

I had blown a great opportunity to harvest a trophy buck!

At dark, I gathered my daypack, emptied my rifle and walked slowly to my truck for the journey back to camp. I was heartbroken.

Relating my story to the members in the camp, I received sympathy, but no cigar. All members feel badly about a colleague missing a trophy buck.

My partner Al shared that he had sighted many does each evening by his hunting stand. He suggested I hunt with him to fill my doe tag. I readily accepted his offer.

Sitting with Al by my side, we talked about future plans, following his recent retirement after 38 years as a professor of education at Central Michigan University in Mt. Pleasant, Michigan. He was going to build a home in Florida – a life-long dream.

We had talked for about 30 minutes when Al suddenly spotted some deer approaching our stand.

Ready with my rifle in hand, I watched the deer approaching.

Snow was falling. The deer approached within 50 yards of the blind.

"I'm going to shoot a large doe to fill my tag," I whispered to Al. We both sat motionless until the deer were in the best position for a shot.

"Get ready," I whispered to Al.

Just before I squeezed the trigger, a large doe turned and ran quickly into swamp grass, as if chasing away a stranger. I immediately suspected more deer were approaching. I turned my scope toward the area where the doe had charged.

Emerging from the swamp grass was a large antlered buck. Walking directly toward me, I steadied the cross-hairs on the chest of the buck and squeezed the trigger. The entire event took only seconds.

"You got him!" exclaimed Al. "He's down."

I emerged from the stand and walked toward the downed buck. He was a beautiful, golden-antlered six-pointer.

Al congratulated me and we laughed together.

How clever of us to be day dreaming about moving south while waiting for the "Florida Buck!"

Dave's Red Hot Chili

Having shot his buck, Dave, who rarely cooks, decided to prepare a camp meal of venison chili.

Not being accustomed to kitchen duty, he nonetheless assured the membership he knew exactly how to prepare chili.

Mixing the ingredients of venison burger, onions, kidney beans and tomatoes, he boiled his mixture with great anticipation of a gourmet hot meal for the hunters when they returned to the camp.

Tasting the mixture, Dave felt it needed more chili powder.

Searching through the cupboard he found some red cayenne pepper he thought would spice-up his mixture.

Placing a liberal amount of the red pepper in the chili, he proceeded to stir and heat the large kettle of savory goodies.

Upon arrival back at camp, members were greeted with a large smile from Dave and the announcement that he had a special dinner ready for their enjoyment.

Spooning large amounts into bowls, Dave served his mixture to all who were hungry.

Several members smacked their lips as they shoveled in the tasty chili.

"Wow!"

"Hot!"

Sweat immediately appeared on the brows of the hunters dining on the hot spicy meal that Dave had prepared with pride.

"What did you put in this chili?" asked several hungry hunters.

"Chili powder," claimed Dave. "Don't you like it?"

In a deer camp you quickly learn not to criticize the cook. He who criticizes cooks the next meal.

"It's good," said Al, sweat pouring from his brow.

"Best chili that I have ever had," Bruce observed.

"Really good," responded Ron.

"Kind of hot," said Jim…"but good!"

"I can't eat anymore," said Dick, as he searched for and then displayed the bottle of chili powder Dave had used for the mixture.

"Aha! You used red cayenne pepper instead of chili powder!" I exclaimed.

At the discovery, we all laughed and immediately voted to dump the remaining chili for the coyotes.

"I tried," said Dave, as he carried the large pot into the woods to discard the fiery mixture for more appreciative pallets.

Big Buck – Wrong Gun

Bob Caltrider, a local road engineer and early Pine Hill Club member, prepared to hit the woods on the fifth morning of the 1986 season. Bob did not yet have his buck and was intent on filling his tag.

Gathering his thermos, shells and flashlight, he grabbed "his" rifle from the camp rack of beloved and well-worn weapons of deer destruction.

Bob hunted with a .30-.30 Winchester Model 94. Many of the Pine Hill Club hunters used this famous timber rifle, as it was popularly known among most hunters at the time, as the "perfect deer rifle."

Returning to camp at 1:00 p.m., Bob announced he had shot a nice eight-point buck. He related his story to the hunters in the cabin. He also noted he had forgotten he had an orange sight on his rifle.

We all celebrated Bob's achievement as a successful hunter.

"You got a really nice buck," I said. "He is a beauty."

Bob beamed with pride over his accomplishments and retold the story about jumping the buck from a small swale and hitting it on the run.

"Great shot," said Joe. "Deer are hard to hit on the run."

Uncle Vern returned to the cabin about 3:00 p.m. He passionately exclaimed someone had his rifle.

"This isn't my gun," complained Vern. "My rifle has an orange sight."

"No," I responded.

"Bob, where is your rifle?" said Joe.

"In my gun case," said Bob

We all gathered around as Bob drew "his" Winchester from the gun case.

"That's my rifle! See the orange sight!" exclaimed Uncle Vern.

Oops! It was a good thing both hunters were using .30-.30's.

Jim Ward's Bunkhouse

One year, a special joke was played on Jim, Ward, Sr., a camp member and retired school superintendent.

Jim had the reputation of being one of the loudest snorers in camp. He could rattle the timbers with the best of the members.

Following several nights of loud snoring, the members decided his talent called for a response.

While Jim was hunting, members moved an old building of four feet by eight feet into the common parking area of the camp. Onto this visible structure, they attached a large sign that read "JIM WARD'S BUNKHOUSE."

Leaving the structure for Jim to find, the members howled with laughter.

Upon Jim's return to the camp, he spotted the large building positioned in the parking area of the camp and near the main cabin. He couldn't help but see the large sign attached.

Entering the cabin, he loudly asked, "Who put the sign on my bunkhouse?"

No one responded.

"What are you talking about Jim?" inquired Ron.

All members, lead by Jim, adjourned outside the cabin to examine the sign and structure.

"You certainly won't disturb anyone in there with your snoring," said Joe.

Jim sputtered a broken response, as members howled with laughter.

After taking pictures of "JIM WARDS' BUNKHOUSE" we returned to the lodge and resumed our euchre game.

Deer camp jokes are many and varied. Good-natured kidding and laughter are vital ingredients in any successful hunting camp. Their role in creating the traditions inherent therein cannot be ignored!

The Arrowhead Buck

Hunting camps, including the Pine Hill Club, are filled with stories
and tall tales about deer hunting and other events of the moment.
However, none are as good as the true stories that actually occur in camp.

Doug McFarlane, a local businessman and camp member, arrived at
the cabin two days before the opening day of the 1998 rifle deer season.
As he burst through the door and loudly interrupted the euchre game in
progress, he excitedly announced that he had just seen something that
we weren't going to believe.

With that announcement all members present rocked back in their
chairs and gave Doug their undivided attention. All anticipated something profound and exotic that could only come from an excited hunter
anxious to share his news.

"Listen," Doug said, "I can't believe what I just saw!"

"South of the gate at the bottom of the hill I saw a six or eight point
buck with an arrow stuck in his head. The buck looked at me for at least
30 seconds. I had a full, clear view of the deer. He's got an orange arrow,
with blue feathers, sticking out of his head. Not a piece of arrow but a
full shaft! A feathered, orange aluminum arrow! The arrow waves with
each turn of the deer's head.

"I just can't believe it," he repeated.

"Amazing," I said as I noted Doug's excitement. "I can't believe a deer
could carry around the full shaft without breaking the arrow on a tree or
piece of brush. I never heard of such a thing.

With Doug's reputation for telling the truth and with an earlier, similar report from Jerry Smith, a local neighbor, we all concluded there
must indeed be a buck running around the camp with an arrow stuck
in its head.

We quickly dubbed the deer "Old Arrowhead."

Thereafter, the stories about sighting "Old Arrowhead" were repeated
many times in the camp.

Most members upon hearing about the sighting would react with,
"Are you sure you weren't drinking when you saw the deer?"

"Did you see any elephants or zebras at the same time?" asked others.

All roared with laughter as Doug responded to the kind of light-
hearted kidding and joking so common in deer camps.

On opening morning, Pine Hill Club members prepared for the hunt. With coffee cup raised high, Doug announced he was going to shoot "Old Arrowhead."

His announcement brought more loud laughter in the camp, as members scurried to leave for their hunting blinds before the first sign of dawn.

On opening day evening, the Pine Hill Club is always a beehive of activity. Hunters bring their bucks to camp and stories of shots missed, deer bagged and funny incidents that occurred during the long day in the field are shared between members.

"I wondered how Doug made out today?" Joe asked, as he hung a nice eight-point buck on the pole with the help of others already in camp.

Ironically, at that moment, Doug's truck pulled into the camp. There was no mistaking from Doug's smile that he had been successful.

"You can always spot the grin of success," I thought to myself.

"Bring your flashlights back here," directed Doug, as he walked to the back of his pick up truck. "Check this out!"

Laying in the back of the truck was a beautiful seven point buck with an arrow deeply imbedded in its skull, just as Doug had described to camp members two days before the season opener.

"I shot him at 9:30 a.m. this morning, coming out of the cedars to the right of my blind. He dropped in his tracks at my first shot," said Doug. "What do you think?"

We all surrounded the deer to check for ourselves.

Member Doug McFarlane with the "Arrowhead buck."

"I can't believe he could carry that arrow for nearly one month without breaking the shaft," I repeated.

Everyone shook their head in amazement.

Together, we hoisted the buck on the pole with arrow still imbedded it it's skull.

Needless to say the arrowhead buck was a major conversation item at the camp that season. Neighbors visiting to view the buck pole stood in awe.

Many pictures were taken recording this unusual event and Doug smiled with pride as he viewed his prize.

Neckties for the hunters

Deer camp tradition is a powerful force affecting both young and old alike. Some rituals become almost sacred as camps, over time, establish many unique ways to do things. These actions often become unwritten rules and form the traditions of the camp. The Pine Hill Club is obviously no different.

One tradition that is annually repeated on the opening night of deer season is a full sit-down dinner, catered by a local family known throughout the area for their outstanding home cooking.

Tom and Carol Biersbach have catered the opening night meal at our camp for many years. This dinner includes chicken, pork and beef with all the trimmings. It is a wonderful feast.

Members and guests at this dinner on the eve of the hunting season are required to wear neckties. If the member or guest doesn't bring a necktie, he selects one from the many garage sale specials hanging from a rack in the corner of the cabin.

This pre-season gathering has become a valued moment when we review camp rules, share announcements from the year past, and hear from members sitting around the dinner table.

We always say a prayer at this meal and ask God for another safe and successful season.

Members sit quietly with neckties flowing from their flannel shirts. Some wear their neckties over sweatshirts or vests. Whatever their attire, all at the table wear neckties.

Following announcements and the recognition of important events in members' lives, a huge meal is served.

After dessert members gather at the end of the cabin for a camp picture. The mood is always festive among the hunters with joking, kidding and good-natured bantering among all present.

Stories get better with time and shortly the card games begin. Usually we have three tables of euchre going at one time with members and guests freely enjoying the game.

Neckties are removed after the picture and another year of camp tradition is hung on the rack.

Front Porch Turkey

Every hunter can relate to the unusual and unpredictable events that surround the pursuit of game. Camp member John Tyler is no exception.

The first day of turkey season a few years ago, John returned to camp. He reported his frustration with an elusive gobbler he had been watching for two weeks prior to the opening day.

John had seen several turkeys in the morning, but all were uncooperative, refusing to respond to his calling efforts.

Frustration with uncooperative turkeys is a common feeling among hunters of the great bearded bird. Turkeys have a way of doing exactly the opposite of what they are expected to do.

After a hot meal and brief discussion of his disappointment with the other members in the camp, John proceeded to stretch out and relax on the front porch of the cabin.

As the sun warmed the day, John fell sound asleep, seated in the rocking chair located on the long porch attached to our cabin.

Suddenly, John was awakened. He looked into the field near the cabin porch. This open area has several rows of pine trees, which border an aspen ridge leading to a long wet swamp.

Suddenly, he spotted a large tom turkey strutting in the open field within fifty yards of the cabin porch.

Immediately and without hesitation John burst into the cabin to quickly announce his findings. By this time and due to his excitement, the turkey had disappeared over the hill and was heading toward the wet swamp that divides our property.

Grabbing his shotgun, turkey calls and camouflage clothes, John rapidly proceeded to circle the area hoping to intercept the large gobbler he had sleepily spotted from the cabin porch.

As we sat in camp laughing about John finally seeing the turkey he'd been hunting so diligently in the field, we heard a single shot from the direction of the swamp.

"Maybe John got his turkey," I announced, in hopes that he had been successful.

"Maybe the turkey got John," quipped Bruce.

We all waited in eager anticipation for John to return and share news with us about his trek.

After a thirty-minute wait, the cabin door flew open and a mud-covered John Tyler burst into the cabin.

"I got my turkey!" John proudly announced. "I got him," he repeated.

"It looks like he got you," I said raising from my chair to hear John's story and view his bird.

"I circled the swamp and called once," said John excitedly. "The turkey responded immediately. He came out where I thought he would and I had one long shot," replied John.

"The gobbler collapsed when I shot, but then he got to his feet and headed for the swamp. I finally caught up to him and wrung his neck."

"Come look at him, he has a 10-11 inch beard," said John.

"Congratulations," I said.

"Great job," said Roger and Dick.

"Beautiful bird," responded Bruce.

John beamed with pride

Roger Dixon with Tom turkey shot during special fall hunt.

and said, "Someone should hunt from the porch tomorrow."

We all laughed and went to get our cameras to record this event.

Fire in the Cabin

As previously described, the original Pine Hill Club cabin was a 12-foot by 16-foot structure. This small building was a crude, cramped, rugged structure, with a propane lantern for light and a vintage wood burner for heat.

Members and guests would pile clothes, boots and cased guns and supplies in every available corner. No space went unused.

The cabin was always crowded with happy hunters. One door and two small windows provided fresh air and sunlight. A small apartment-sized propane gas stove was used to prepare food and the lingering smell of bacon grease permeated everything in the cabin.

Though crowded, smelly and filled with smoke, the cabin was home to our enthusiastic hunters. Wet socks drying, long johns airing, and the wood burner smoking created an atmosphere that was truly a castle setting for our serious deer hunters.

Wood to stoke the fire was brought inside the cabin and stacked near the antique stove. The cabin provided shelter from the cold wind that whistled around the long stovepipe extending through the ceiling.

One opening night, with the fire blazing, lantern turned off and stomachs full of hot food, snoring soon commenced as members quickly went to sleep, dreaming of the large buck they hoped to kill the next morning.

At about 11:00 p.m., Chuck Pisoni suddenly woke to find a smoke-filled cabin. He yelled loudly to awaken the other hunters as he searched for the origin of the smoke.

Flashlights quickly appeared as sleepy hunters investigated the problem.

For a long moment concern was high and thoughts frantic, as members searched to see if in fact the cabin was burning.

In retrospect the atmosphere was one of a comedy.

Groggy hunters attired in long johns, stumbled clumsily about the cabin, tripping over boots, clothes, and boxes.

Thankfully, the problem was a simple one. Wood stacked by the stove had fallen on the side of the hot wood burner. The wood pieces were smoldering, causing smoke to circulate throughout the cabin. Throwing the charred wood outside, we proceeded to check the entire stove area for sparks. We confirmed the wood against the stove was the cause of the problem.

With the problem solved, I re-checked the stove, fanned the remaining smoke from the cabin and thankfully returned to my bed.

After a quarter of a century of camp operation, veteran members still laugh about the "fire in the cabin."

Such memories form the basis of the camp history and tradition. We were all truly thankful nothing more serious than a frightening awakening had occurred. However, we were careful not to pile wood near the stove on future evenings.

Enough said! Lesson learned!

Wrong Shells – Right Gun

When Gary Walters, a businessman from Grand Rapids, arrived at camp he announced he was a guest of Al Quick. All members welcomed Gary to the camp and invited him into the cabin to have a cool drink.

Gary was a novice hunter but he displayed enthusiasm about the possibility of tagging a whitetail buck. He was eager to learn about the camp and truly enjoyed the atmosphere presented by veteran hunters willing to share stories about previous hunts.

I explained that all members of the Pine Hill Club are asked to remain in their blinds for opening two days of season. No member is allowed to walk around the woods as walking scares the deer and often interferes with other hunters waiting patiently for an elusive buck.

Gary was most cooperative and reported he didn't want to break any rules as a non-member in the camp. He was warmly welcomed by all and quickly engaged in the card games and pre-season activities of getting ready to hunt.

All members are anxious to get in the woods on opening morning and Gary was no exception.

He was assigned to hunt the Buckhorn blind, which is about one-quarter mile from the cabin. Ron Williams had volunteered to walk with him to his stand and show him how to light his stove and get settled in for the hunt.

I asked Gary on opening morning if he had shells, knew the rules about walking around and was ready to shoot a big buck. He assured me he had bought a new box of shells to use in the borrowed rifle he carried and was really prepared to get a deer.

Again, I reminded him that he should not leave his blind and walk around on opening day. He assured me he would stay put in his stand, unless he shot a buck.

I wished him well as he left the cabin for the short walk to his stand.

At dark, when I returned to the cabin I observed Gary sitting at the table. He had just arrived and anxiously reported that he had seen several deer at his stand.

"How did it go?" I asked.

"You won't believe what happened to me," he responded. "I tried to load my rifle when I was in my stand only to find that I had bought the wrong shells."

"Why didn't you walk back to the cabin and get some shells for your rifle?" I retorted.

"I didn't want to walk around in the woods, as you said," he replied.

I laughed and asked, "Did you sit all day without shells for your rifle?"

"Yes", he said, with a sheepish grin.

The next day I personally checked to see that Gary had the right shells for his rifle.

Camp members still laugh about this event, which occurred over twenty years ago. This type of story is what memories in a deer camp are made of. All agree, beginners usually can make the most mistakes.

Gary learned a very important lesson about deer hunting on that fateful day. Simply put, be certain you have the right shells for your rifle.

I hope these true stories about our camp will bring back some memories of your past hunts. In any case, you know more about our members and the events that have occurred at the Pine Hill Club.

CHAPTER 6

Tracking Wounded Deer

*V*eteran and novice deer hunters alike share many common challenges in the woods. One of the most daunting of these is tracking and recovering a wounded whitetail. This section is designed to share some tips and tricks I have learned over the past five decades of hunting whitetail deer.

Many factors contribute to successfully locating and recovering wounded deer. While some of these variables are beyond your control, most are not. If you are going to consistently locate wounded game, you must master those skills and factors you can control.

Whitetail deer have an unbelievable capacity to flee danger, even when fatally wounded. The animals seemingly draw on almost supernatural powers to escape and are capable of running long distances after being shot, even with high-powered rifles.

Hunters, by following some basic rules of tracking, can recover the majority of such critically wounded animals.

As discussed in the section on the best deer rifles, a hunter who can shoot accurately and with confidence minimizes the need to make long tracks to recover game. There is absolutely no substitute for accurate shot placement!

Regrettably, accurate shot placement is often impacted by adverse weather conditions, running game, dense brush and foliage, or other factors beyond the control of the hunter. Buck fever is an added malady that can affect both the novice and veteran hunter, given the right set of circumstances.

Therefore, all hunters — both veterans and beginners — will at times experience poor shot placement or miss their shot. A graduate degree in tracking skills becomes critical at these moments.

The basics of locating wounded game fall into several essential steps that absolutely must be followed, if these animals are to be consistently recovered. These steps, as discussed in this chapter, should be viewed in their totality, not singularly.

The guidelines apply equally well to rifle, bow, and muzzle-loader hunters. Weather conditions may mandate minor changes, but the fundamentals are always the same.

Recovering of wounded game is the goal!

Step # 1.

Always Note the Reaction of the Deer to the Shot

Did the deer hunch, drop, bolt, stumble, jerk or give some visible sign of being hit?

A fatally wounded deer will often flinch at the shot and may stagger or fall, only to regain its feet and run off, following the shot.

Deer hit in the stomach or intestine usually "hunch" up or "buckle" in the middle. Both front and rear feet usually touch when the deer hunches in reaction to the shot.

Weather permitting, you should not push the track of such a wounded deer. Let it lie down and die. If you rush your track, you can push the deer out of the area and lose it. A gut shot deer requires some different tracking technique than one hit in the lungs.

Most deer will visibly react when being hit

Jamie Dixon with nice buck he shot opening day.

71

with either a bullet or an arrow. This observation provides critical information, as your track will depend heavily on such data.

Before beginning any track, I always ask the hunter to describe, in specific detail, what the deer did when it was shot. It is not uncommon for a fatally wounded deer to show no immediate signs of being hit.

Recall your sight picture! Were the cross hairs on the deer's shoulder, chest, or neck? Did you rush your shot or take careful aim? Was the deer moving when you shot? Is your gun or bow sighted to shoot accurately? Did you flinch? How long did you watch the deer?

Always ask the hunter or yourself, what did the deer do when you fired your rifle or released the arrow?

Answers to these basic questions provide a blueprint for tracking the deer. If the hunter doesn't know where he aimed at the deer, this lack of knowledge can severely limit a tracker's ability to locate the animal. Knowing where a deer was hit allows a tracker to proceed with a basic understanding about the potential impact of the hit.

STEP # 2.
Watch the Deer as Long as You Can, Noting the Direction It Runs, and Listen

This guideline sounds far simpler than it actually is for the hunter in the field. Some hunters get so excited they can't identify which direction the deer ran. This is especially true if the buck is with other deer. For instance, you often get a "popcorn" effect from lots of whitetails exploding in all directions.

I once guided a hunter who shot a nice buck walking alone in the hardwoods. The frustrated shooter claimed the deer fell down, but he didn't remember the direction the deer ran. However, he was absolutely positive that the deer ran south.

I proceeded to search for one hour in that direction.

Not finding blood or any sign of a hit, I decided to circle north. I found the deer within 100 yards. To this day the hunter still is convinced that the deer ran south.

In a similar vein, use your ears as well as your eyes to help determine where your deer is headed. Listen to the fleeing animal. Is the deer splashing in water or breaking through brush? Is it moving well or is it stumbling into trees and brush? All these clues help locate the deer's direction and the impact of the hit.

You must do your very best to note the "line" or direction the deer took following your shot. This information is extremely critical before beginning your track. Following a wounded deer in the wrong direction is frustrating and unproductive. Be sure you know the proper direction of the fleeing animal!

STEP # 3.
Note the Exact Position of the Deer When You Made Your Shot
Where was the deer standing? Was the deer broadside, angling toward you, or walking away?

It is critically important to recall the exact position where the deer was standing or moving when you fired. This is a key reference point for the track. This vital information allows you to better understand the location of the hit and serves as a guidepost for beginning your track.

A deer standing broadside to the hunter should show some visible sign of a hit. Additionally, the kill zone is much greater when the animal is broadside, as compared to walking toward you or quartering away.

STEP # 4.
Begin Your Search at the Spot Where You Shot at the Deer
This also sounds simple, but many hunters fail to locate the spot where they first shot their deer.

Never race wildly to the location where you think the deer was when you shot. You could alter needed sign of the hit and eliminate critical information that will help you making a successful track.

Relax. Walk calmly and slowly to the area, noting where you were when you shot and locate where the deer was when you fired or released the arrow. Mark this spot for future reference.

Look carefully for hair, blood, bone, or tracks on the snow or ground. Snow makes for much easier tracking; however, even with good tracking snow, if you rush the track, you can lose a fatally hit deer.

Hard hit deer won't always leave a clear blood trail. High lung shots for example, leave only small flecks of red at the beginning of a blood trail. Later, when the lungs fill, larger drops and/or spraying will often result in a much clearer trail … if you haven't lost it by rushing the track.

Always note if the deer fell down, stumbled or made some other signs of being hit. Be very observant of the area where you shot your deer for vital signs telling you the extent of the shot.

Again, always approach the area where you shot the deer with extreme caution. By being patient, you will not destroy vital clues as to where the deer was hit or the impact of the shot.

STEP # 5.

At the Point Where You Initially Hit the Deer, Look for Hair, Blood or Some Other visible Sign of a Hit. Mark the Spot With a Handkerchief or Orange Marking Tape

Whenever I find blood, bone or hair, I quickly mark the spot with my handkerchief or some orange marking tape carried for that purpose. Such a marker serves as an important point of reference, if you lose the track. It can also help establish a line of travel taken by a wounded animal.

STEP # 6.

Look for Your Arrow and Wait!

Bow hunters should always look for their arrow. The signs on that arrow serve as critical evidence of a vital hit.

Bow hunters should wait a minimum of two hours before starting a track on a deer.

Never rush a deer that has been shot with an arrow. The only exception to this rule is if it is raining and the sign might be washed away. At the Pine Hill Club, we discourage bow hunting in rainy weather. The rain can quickly wash away a trail, resulting in a wasted buck. Among the sins of hunting, this one walks to the forefront.

Many hunters fail to wait after shooting the animal, making it flee. Don't push a bow-shot deer! We say at the Pine Hill Club that, "When they are dead, they are dead for a long time."

I believe the biggest single mistake a bow hunter can make is to rush the track of a bow-shot deer. Such haste often destroys vital tracking sign and makes the animal run even deeper into heavy cover, and almost always has an adverse affect on the chances of recovering a wounded animal.

STEP # 7.

Always Note the Type of Sign You Have on the Ground

Grass, corn and/or other stomach matter in the trail are all indicators of a gut shot deer.

Do you have dark red blood, which indicates a possible liver shot, or bright red blood, which often means a possible lung shot?

Are the bubbles in the blood a possible lung shot?

Is the blood "spraying" on both sides of the track indicating a possible lung shot or are there just little spots of red on the grass or ferns, which indicates a possible superficial wound or even a high lung shot.

Is there blood on the trees? What is the location of blood on the trees? Note the height of the blood sign on the trees or ferns, which should help indicate the position of the hit.

Is the deer stumbling? This is often an indication of a critically wounded animal. Is the sign in a straight line or zigzagging? Staggering movement could indicate a fatally wounded deer, struggling to seek safety, but mortally wounded resulting in the faltering movement.

Every clue helps tell the hunter the extent and location of the hit. This information is critically important in finding a wounded deer.

Good shot placement usually results in a good blood trail! A deer hit in the lungs will not go far, especially if left for two hours. Good blood will result in a mortally wounded deer, if the shot is through the chest, femoral artery, heart, lungs, or liver. As discussed earlier, sometimes deer bleed internally and do not open up until about 100 yards into the track. Any deer critically hit will not travel far if left alone for two hours. Usually a fatally hit deer will lie down in a relatively short while, if not pushed. It will then bleed out, resulting in a quick and successful track by the hunter.

If you track over 100 yards and begin to lose the blood trail, consider marking the spot and leaving the track for a few more hours. If you push such a track, the deer will often continue running deeper into heavy cover, leaving you little or no sign to follow.

The decision to wait longer or not will often be a judgement call. In my experience, it is much better to wait two extra hours than to continue pushing a deer with poor shot placement.

STEP # 8.

Move Slowly on the Blood Trail

Hunters on a blood trail who move rapidly often miss critical signs left by a wounded deer. For example, you can easily walk past a stained fern or a blood-marked tree that will indicate a change in direction of the deer. The result will be a lost buck and no venison on the pole.

All hunters are anxious to find their deer. This eagerness, however, can lead to mistakes that destroy critical tracking sign. The loss in such situations will be your fault. If you have a poor trail, get off your track and get help.

Two or three hunters are much better at tracking than one individual. Regardless, if you are alone or with other hunters, you must always proceed slowly on the trail.

Mark Day kneels by buck pole on third day of rifle season.

Begin your track by making small circles in the direction the deer ran from the point of your initial shot. Until you locate first blood and can establish, without doubt, the direction the deer is running, be very cautious and slow on the track. Mark every sign of blood, hair or bone to establish a line. This can be done with orange marking tape or even a handkerchief torn into small strips. Tie the markers on a branch located at eye level or higher. Don't put the markers too low, as you will not be able to see them when you try to retrace your steps to find last blood.

On several tracks I have used pieces of my shirt, hat or coat to mark a spot. It is critically important to mark the sign, especially if you are trailing a poorly hit deer.

If you are tracking with another hunter, you should post him at the last blood, moving him forward as new sign is found. Again, it is important to mark the sign, even if you are tracking with another hunter. This allows you to retrace your steps should you lose the trail of the wounded deer.

Never walk on the blood trail, as you can easily destroy important sign you may need to return to later. If you have blood, hair, or bone always walk beside, never on, such sign to avoid losing critical clues you may need again.

STEP # 9.
Always Watch Ahead for the Wounded Deer

At times you will jump a wounded deer. Observing the animal at such a moment can provide an indication of how hard the deer has been hit. Using this information, you can better determine whether to continue the track or decide to mark the sign and leave the track for one or two hours.

Sometimes at dark, especially in cool weather, you should make the decision to leave the wounded deer alone until the next morning. Patience usually will assist you in finding the deer. Delaying such tracks has helped us find many poorly hit deer at the Pine Hill Club.

STEP # 10.
Don't Kid Yourself about Your Shot Placement

If you don't find hair, blood or any visible sign of a hit within 50 or 100 yards of where you believe you hit the deer, you probably missed it! If the deer didn't react or indicate a hit, again, you probably missed the deer.

This may not always be the case, but failure to find any sign of a hit is pretty darn good indicator of a miss.

As noted earlier, bow hunters should look carefully for their arrow. A clean recovered arrow, with no sign of hair, blood or intestinal fluid, is a clear indicator of a miss.

I always smell a recovered arrow in an attempt to detect any strong odors of intestine or stomach content.

Not finding an arrow after a shot may mean you hit the deer and the arrow remained in the animal. This almost always means a hard track, due to the lack of a good blood trail.

Always work your way toward the exact route of the fleeing deer. Be honest with yourself. After searching for at least an hour without finding any sign, you should admit you have probably missed the deer.

A wounded deer will usually (not every time) show signs of a hit within the first 50 yards of the trail after the shot. If you cannot find any sign of a hit, you obviously have nothing to follow.

When this happens, you should circle and carefully search for sign. However, if you find nothing to confirm a wounded deer after a conscientious search, don't damage your hunting area by aimlessly walking around in the woods and leaving human scent scattered throughout the area.

STEP # 11.
Tracking a Deer is Like Solving a Puzzle

Each small sign gives you more information, leading to a final solution and recovery of the deer. Every broken branch, bloodstained fern, or mark on the ground from a stumbling deer adds to the solution of the tracking and finding a wounded animal.

An added clue that has helped some of the Pine Hill Club hunters

when rain or a poor blood trail has resulted in a lost track: watch for concentrations of crows or ravens. These scavengers will flock to a dead deer, seeking a free meal. Our hunters have found more than one deer that would have been lost without the help of these feathered guides.

Remember the previous steps when tracking wounded deer. Go slowly, mark your trail and be patient. Such efforts will usually put venison on the table and reward you with a trophy on the buck-pole.

GOOD LUCK!

Author with bow killed buck.

CHAPTER 7

Memorable Tracks at the Pine Hill Club

We have had many excellent and memorable tracks at the Pine Hill Club over the years. Hopefully sharing some of these tracks, where we used the concepts discussed in the previous chapter on "Tracking Wounded Deer" will help other hunters successfully locate wounded deer.

I believe you will enjoy and learn something from reading about these challenging tracks at our camp.

TRACK # 1. Bert's Buck

Bert Palmer is a veteran hunter at the Pine Hill Club. In his professional life, he served as a detective for the Isabella County Sheriff's Department prior to his retirement in 2000. He is a good shot and a very patient member of our deer camp, hunting from his favorite stand, day after day throughout each rifle season.

On the evening of November 20, 1989, he shot a fat buck just before dark. He was hunting in a large cedar swamp in the center of the property.

Knowing he had hit the deer he waited until dark, marked first blood and returned to the cabin for help. After he explained in detail what had happened, I was convinced we would find the animal.

With lanterns and flashlights ready, we waited a full hour before returning to the cedar swamp to recover the buck. With Bert at my side, we walked to his blind and once again reviewed his shot.

"Where was the deer standing and exactly what happened when you fired at it?" I asked Bert.

Moving to the area where he had wounded the buck, I found a small amount of hair and a tiny drop of blood. Properly marking the spot for future reference, I began the slow process of tracking the wounded buck.

Bert remained in place beside the last blood, while we proceeded to crawl through the dense cedars and blow downs. Limited blood and a dark moonless sky made the tracking slow and challenging.

After two hours of hard work we had only traveled approximately 100 yards. Intermittent strips of blaze orange tape marked the spots where we had found blood. It became increasingly apparent from the lack of bright red blood that the buck had been gut shot.

Bert and I discussed the situation and decided not to push the deer, but to wait for daylight to resume the track.

Cedar swamps are very tough places to track a wounded animal at anytime as the branches and blow downs present unusually difficult challenges for a hunter negotiating walking space. Additionally, if the deer were indeed gut shot, it should be allowed time to die and not be pushed even further into the swamp.

We marked the last blood and left the woods with high hopes of recovering the deer the next morning.

At first light the following day, Bert and I drove back to the cedar swamp to search for the wounded animal.

Locating our last orange marker, we studiously began to search for blood and sign.

Minuscule, infrequent drops of blood, unfound in the evening darkness the day before, provided us with a line-of-sight trail. Within 50 yards of our last blood mark from the night before, we found the dead buck.

It was a nice spike-horn! As we had suspected, the shot had not been a good lung hit, but had struck farther back in the body cavity than desired.

After field dressing and tagging the deer, we triumphantly dragged the buck to the truck. It was a fitting ending to a most successful track. Had we pushed the deer the night before, we probably would have lost both the track and the deer.

The lesson is clear: Never push a wounded deer while tracking it, especially if you suspect it might be gut shot.

TRACK # 2. Dave's Deer

Dave Mills, on a sunny October morning, returned to camp to report that he had shot a deer from his bow stand. According to Dave's reports, the deer reacted to the shot, heading for a water-covered swamp created by a small colony of beavers. This area is one comprising the most difficult terrain on the Pine Hill Club property, featuring heavy brush, deep water and clinging muck.

I quizzed Dave about the shot. He assured me he had hit the deer and it carried his arrow. Waiting until noon, roughly four hours from the time of the shot, Dave, member John Tyler and I proceeded to the spot where Dave had arrowed the deer.

I wore hip boots, because of the water in the beaver pond. Locating blood on the leaves, I ventured into the swamp. John and Dave remained on high ground as I proceeded through the mucky swamp noting any slight sign of blood left by the wounded animal.

Marking the sign with strips from my handkerchief, I did not believe the deer would go far in the water. I advanced with caution!

I was wrong on two counts! First, the depth of the chilly water quickly exceeded the height of my hip boots. Fall rains had been greater than I estimated. Second, the deer had gone much farther

Dave Mills and eight point buck shot with bow.

than I had anticipated, proving once again to me the unbelievable endurance of a whitetail deer.

John and Dave joked with me as I slopped around in the cattails and brush. After fruitlessly searching for over 100 yards, I knew I needed help. I couldn't follow the track without assistance.

I called to them to wade into the swamp and help me continue the search.

The three of us then waded into the ever deeper swamp, looking for the wounded animal. The extra trackers provided critical and necessary coverage and we were able to continue following the deer's faint trail. At times, we were in water up to our waists. We trailed the wounded deer by blood marks left on the sides of brush that grew out of the swamp.

Finally, after struggling through a long 100 yards of poor sign and chilling swamp, I spotted the deer on a high hummock at the edge of the beaver swamp. The buck was still alive but in poor condition. I quickly dispatched the animal by cutting its throat.

> *Note: Hunters should exercise extreme care when approaching any wounded animal. Given the opportunity,.a finishing shot to the neck with either an arrow or bullet, as appropriate to the season, is far safer than this method, which was used only as a last resort. We had no other weapons with us on this wet, difficult swamp track.*

Dragging the deer took over an hour of exhausting effort before we finally spotted the road and were back in friendly territory.

Following some not altogether humorous kidding about "Don't ever shoot a deer near water again," we finally hung Dave's deer on the camp buck pole. Changing into dry clothes and relaxing over a cool drink, we reviewed our watery track.

TRACK # 3. Jim Sr.'s Buck

Jim Ward, Sr. shot a nicely racked buck just before dark on November 19, 1998. Jim was sitting in Al Quick's blind, as Al had taken a buck earlier in the season and had already left camp in anticipation of moving to Florida for the winter months.

When Jim returned to camp to report shooting the deer, he marked the time at 5:35 p.m. The light had been fading rapidly, but the buck's antlers had showed brightly in his scope. He was certain of a good hit.

Jim shoots a 30-06 caliber, Browning auto-loading rifle. Though in his seventies, Jim displays the vitality and energy of a much younger hunter. He is the camp storyteller par excellence.

Several members of the camp gave Jim some friendly kidding, such as, "Are you sure it was a buck?"

"Are you sure you shot a deer?"

"Did the deer go 'Moo' when you shot?"

"Don't kid yourself, guys, I shot a good buck," responded Jim. "Now, help me find it."

Our camp manager, Bruce Anderson, member John Tyler and I are all veteran trackers. We readily volunteered to assist Jim in locating his deer.

A slow, steady rain was falling, so we immediately prepared for the track. Lanterns, flashlights and marking tape were collected as we proceeded to the area where Jim had shot the buck.

When we arrived at his stand, we again asked Jim to fully explain where the deer was when he fired at it, how it reacted to the shot and which direction the deer had run afterwards. Working in the growing darkness and soft rain, Jim gave us the best account he could and we proceeded to the spot where he believed he had hit the deer.

The light from the lanterns glistened in the drizzling rain off the ferns and blades of grass near the swamp. Intermittent drops of blood were discovered and John and Bruce were immediately on the track. I posted on the last blood, reassuring a concerned Jim that we would find his buck, if it were possible to do so.

As the two veteran deer hunters worked forward seeking signs to follow, I again reflected on the fact that tracking is a science and patience is a virtue all deer hunters must cultivate.

Bruce and John worked the track slowly, moving back and forth in their search for infrequent drops of blood. We covered a long 100 yards in approximately 20 minutes.

With John at the point, the faint blood trail led the trackers in a northeast direction. After repeated, frustrating false trails, we discovered the deer had entered a birch-wooded corner of the property. We finally

Father and son — Jim Ward Sr. and Jim Ward Jr. pose for picture in cabin.

located the buck, piled up approximately 175 yards from where Jim had first shot. The buck was a wide-racked eight-point trophy, and we all celebrated in the soft, drizzling rain.

After tagging and gutting the deer, we dragged the buck to the truck and returned to the cabin to triumphantly hang Jim's deer on the buck-pole.

Hearing my truck, all members in camp came outside to congratulate Jim and to view his deer.

TRACK # 4. Roger's Buck

Roger Dixon, a veteran Pine Hill Club archer, arrowed a fat fork-horned buck on a warm October evening three days into the 1997 Michigan bow season. The shot was made just before dark. Roger saw the deer approach his stand through a cattail swamp. He waited for a broadside shot.

When the buck turned and dropped his head to eat freshly dropped acorns, Roger drew his bow, anchored and released the arrow. The deer leaped, wheeled and ran toward the cattails leading into a large cedar swamp that runs for nearly a mile to the north of the Pine Hill Club property.

Being a veteran bow hunter, Roger waited until dark, cautiously climbed down from his tree stand and looked for his arrow. Knowing he had hit the deer solidly, he was surprised not to find his arrow near the spot of the initial hit. He did find blood in the ferns and knew that he had arrowed the buck hard. Marking the spot of the hit, Roger returned to the camp to report on his hunt and get help with the track.

After describing his shot to me, I was convinced that we would find his deer.

Waiting the minimum two hours as we normally do with a bow-shot deer, we prepared for the track by checking propane levels in the lanterns and getting rope and marking tape. Bruce, John and I were in the camp and readily volunteered to help Roger track the buck.

Although he had shot a nice six-point buck from that stand the previous year, to say that Roger was excited would be an understatement of fact. Beginning and veteran hunters alike get pumped in anticipation of finding a wounded deer. Roger was no exception!

When the excitement stops, a hunter should consider quitting the sport of hunting and take photographs of the deer.

All hunters were equally excited for Roger, as we drove my truck near the blind where he had arrowed the buck.

Lighting the lanterns and readying our flashlights, we proceeded to the point of the shot. We immediately found blood and the track was on.

I took the point while John, Bruce and Roger scanned the ferns for signs of blood. The cattails quickly revealed signs of a good blood trail. We found the broken arrow, covered with bright red blood, about 20 yards from the point of the original shot. Moving slowly, we all pressed forward, with Roger posting on the spot of last blood.

The ferns near the swamp had been coated with tiny drops of blood that appeared to be spraying from a lung shot deer. This blood was bright red and speckled on the leafy ferns. When we hit the cattails in the swamp, heavy blood and a wide deer trail made the tracking much easier for the hunters. The red splotches were on both sides of the well-worn trail leading toward the cedar swamp.

Moving into the cedar swamp and marking the heavy blood trail high on the cattails on both sides of the track, I remarked that the deer was clearly lung shot and would not go far. We would soon find the buck.

Watching ahead, I slowly moved forward, peering into the darkness while looking for the downed deer. In a matter of minutes, I spotted a telltale patch of brown and white.

"There he is!" I exclaimed.

A nice four-pointer lay on the pine needled floor of the cedar swamp. The deer was the reward for our skills as trackers.

Needless to say, Roger was ecstatic and following the customary hugs, pats on the back and congratulations, the work of field dressing the deer and dragging it back to my truck commenced. I held the lantern while Roger gutted his buck.

We all returned to the camp to celebrate Roger's success.

The four tracks discussed above are only a few brief examples of the successful tracks at the Pine Hill Club. I could have written about many others.

I could have also shared some bad news stories of tracks when we did not locate a deer. Although rare, this does occasionally occur.

A true deer hunter never forgets the feeling of loneliness and loss experienced in not recovering a wounded animal. These are the thoughts that haunt your dreams.

Like all good deer hunters, we use all our cumulative skill and knowledge to make a successful track. To do less than our best would truly be a sin against nature.

It is a great feeling to recover a wounded deer and one I hope to repeat many times at our deer camp.

Hopefully, the hints and ideas shared in this book will help you be as successful as we have been over the years at the Pine Hill Club.

Roger Dixon preparing biscuit and gravy breakfast.

CHAPTER 8

Fifty Tips for Bagging a Trophy Buck

$\mathcal{E}$xperts vary in their opinions regarding the best ways to achieve hunting success; however, there are many common elements. In this chapter, we will share advice and information we have garnered over the years while hunting whitetail deer at the Pine Hill Club.

I can guarantee both the beginner and veteran hunter that incorporating these hunting tips into your efforts afield will make you more successful in your pursuit of the whitetail deer.

These suggestions, though certainly not all-inclusive, will serve as a basic guide, helping increase your chances of bagging an illusive trophy.

Further information about successfully hunting deer can be found in two wonderful books by Richard P. Smith from Marquette, Michigan: *Great Michigan Deer Tales, Book 1* and *Great Michigan Deer Tales, Book 2*. These are superb stories, meticulously accounting for the largest bucks taken in Michigan. I highly recommend these books to any deer hunter interested in learning more about successful deer hunting.

The tips shared in this chapter are a result of many years of deer hunting, guiding and working as a longtime owner of a deer camp. The tips are not listed in priority order, but should be taken in their totality. I guarantee you will find these ideas and suggestions helpful and useful on future hunts.

TIP # 1.

Scout your hunting area

Successful hunters spend time in their hunting area well in advance of the season. They look for runways, scrapes and rubs that show bucks are actually in the area, as well as where they are moving.

Deer normally follow the same pattern, moving from bedding area to feeding area. Knowing where the whitetails move in your area gives you a tremendous advantage on opening day. Once the deer are pushed or extreme hunting pressure invades the deer's natural environment, such patterned movement rapidly becomes a thing of the past.

I have found deer tend to use the same runway, year after year. Weather and wind direction can alter the deer's pattern, but their routine is generally the same. Deer are truly creatures of habit. Use this information to your advantage.

TIP # 2.

Sight in your rifle to shoot accurately

This sounds simple and it is. Nonetheless, every season many hunters have an opportunity to kill a deer only to miss the shot because they did not properly sight in their rifle.

All hunters at the Pine Hill Club shoot their rifle well before season. They know where their rifles are hitting at various targets and distances. Even with all this practice and preparation, there is still no guarantee a hunter will hit everything he shoots at in the woods. However, proper preparation, practice and sighting in a weapon significantly improve your odds for a successful hunt.

Easy shots missed are usually the result of not having your gun sighted in or from rushing your shot due to excitement, a lack of patience, or good old-fashioned buck fever.

We discourage any extra noise or movement around camp for two weeks before the opening day of rifle season, so many of our hunters

Uncle Vern, myself, Al Quick and Bert Palmer by buckpole.

Jake Mills, grandson of author, admires buck his daddy shot.

Entrance gate on the farm to the Pine Hill Club.

Geraldine sits in background of butcher shop in front of cabin.

Ed Reihl and author display a plaque in memory of "Pappa Joe".

Tom Peters and Doug McFarlane direct members on wood cutting day.

Camp members smile during break in wood cutting.

Jim Ward, Sr. with bucks hanging.

Author (Bob Mills) stands next to buck pole on second day of season.

Ron Williams knows he has a good hand in euchre.

New addition to the hunting cabin.

Camp members pose for picture opening night – note neckties.

Jim Ward Sr. asking his dog Ginger for advice at card game.

Camp members gather around buck pole following opening day.

Bob Mills and Chuck Pisoni admire large buck on pole.

Neighbor Jerry Smith tells about the arrowhead buck.

Dave Mills shows young son need for gun safety.

Pine Hill Club cabin.

Two Pine Hill
Club bucks
hang in garage
at camp.

Guests pose
for picture with
author in front
of cabin.

Roger Dixon and
Neale Spender cut
up venison on deer
processing day.

Pheasants shot on
opening day lined
up on picnic table
at camp.

Bruce Anderson
gets ready to track
a bow shot buck

Bruce Anderson with nice eight pointer shot on opening day of season.

Members pose for 20th anniversary of camp.

Camp members take a break from wood cutting.

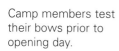

Roger Dixon with Tom turkey shot during special fall hunt.

Camp members test their bows prior to opening day.

Author next to
his hunting blind.

Guests pose for
picture with Dave
Mills (holding
camera) in cabin.

Pine Hill Club
cabin with wood
cut ready for fall
hunting season.

Litter of German
Short Hair puppies
from Ginger.

Doug McFarlane,
son Garren and
Jim Engler beside
pheasants shot
at camp.

Member Wayne Coston with large eight pointer shot opening day.

Author admires nice buck with three sons. (Note beard)

Roger Dixon
with his best
buck ever.

Geoff Quick with
his eight point buck
shot opening day.

Stone fireplace
in cabin. Rocks
came from Pine
Hill Club property.

Jim Ward Sr. and
Wayne Coston
laugh about the big
buck that got away.

Colors at woods on
Pine Hill Club property.

Joe Mills admires his
buck shot on the
third day of season.

Member John Tyler checks the sights on his rifle.

double check the accuracy of their weapons at local ranges immediately before the season begins.

TIP # 3.
Be prepared to wait long hours on your hunting stand

Successful hunters often pack a lunch, take coffee or soda and carry a backpack to their hunting area. The issue of clothing and necessary equipment will be addressed in a separate section of this book. Having such creature comforts available helps hunters remain patiently and quietly at their stands during the long hours in the woods, especially on opening day.

Hunters, who are fidgety, impatient or can't sit quietly, usually help those hunters who can.

Despite stories to the contrary, it is nearly impossible for a hunter to walk up on an alert deer and get a good shot. The deer usually hears you, spots you and presents you with a flag-up signal that they know you are in their area.

Walking up on a deer on dry ground is even more difficult. In fact, it

DEER CAMP — AN AMERICAN TRADITION

is almost impossible. Although a few talented and experienced hunters can successfully stalk whitetail deer, it is a skill that requires special abilities few sportsmen possess.

My experience, after years in the woods, is you are far better served to locate a good runway and wait patiently for deer to appear. Let them come to you.

Soft, rainy conditions or a wet, quiet snow clearly enhance a hunter's chances for a successful stalk. Regardless, my overwhelming preference and advice is to stay put and wait. This will allow you increased opportunities to see deer without their flags flying and clearly provide you with better shooting choices. It is a much-preferred method used by successful hunters.

TIP #4.

Use an odor masking scent cover

Deer have a phenomenal capacity to detect odors. They are the masters of the woods and intimately know their habitat. Strange odors mean danger! One whiff of a human will often send them into hiding, especially the wise, heavily racked bucks we so desire. A deer snorting or blowing nearby is a good indicator you have been scented. It is not a pleasant sound for hopeful hunters.

Good quality scent covers are available at most sporting goods stores. I religiously use TINKS #69 – Doe in Heat. I also spray my clothes with a cover-up scent to help prevent body order from getting to the deer.

Additionally, several sporting stores today carry "Scent-Lok" type clothing. A number of hunters, especially bow hunters, swear by these products.

Whatever scent system or combination of systems you use, you must always be conscious of a deer's capacity to smell. Carelessness in this regard is self-defeating and will often result in an unsuccessful hunt.

TIP # 5.

Silence is golden

As noted in Tip # 4, deer have a tremendous ability to detect strange odors. Whitetail also have excellent hearing. The slightest strange noise can send a deer running for thick cover.

Wear quiet clothing when hunting. Wool or polar fleece are my favorites. Nylon and many other synthetics are usually scratchy sounding and will often signal your presence to wary deer.

Don't bump your gun, bang your binoculars, or clink your thermos, as these sounds will frequently spook deer. Rattling lunch bags, candy wrappers, or shells will also serve to frighten the whitetail. Any unnatural noise can quickly destroy your dreams of a successful hunt.

Silence is my Golden Rule of deer hunting!

TIP # 6.
Keep movement to a minimum

Deer also have exceptional visual acuity! Don't constantly stand-up, sit down, or move around in your deer stand.

Minimize even your head movement! Let your eyes move to check runways and deer movement areas. Move your head slowly, not rapidly, to help avoid being spotted by the deer.

If you see a deer approaching, "Freeze!" Move only when the deer looks the other way or put his head down to feed.

Don't pick up your gun when the deer is looking straight at you. This simple movement will almost always spook a whitetail.

Remember that big bucks don't get that way by being dumb! Trophy bucks are almost always on full alert. Keep any movement in the woods to a minimum.

TIP # 7.
Pick your shot carefully

When you decide to take a shot, be certain of both the position of the animal and of possible branches between you and the deer.

Deer walking toward you or away from you present limited target areas where you can place your shot in a kill zone. A deer turned broadside provides you with both an increased choice of spots to shoot and a larger target area in which to place a fatal shot.

If possible, wait until the deer walks into an opening, without branches or twigs between you and the deer. Even the smallest branch can deflect a bullet and cause you to miss a lifetime trophy.

At times, the deer may not cooperate immediately. Be patient! Many novice hunters rush their shot, resulting in a missed or wounded deer.

Deer moving slowly through the woods often pause and check the area for danger. If your deer hasn't spotted you, scented you or heard you, the chances are excellent it will offer you a good shot. Be patient!

Pick your shot carefully, if you want to put venison on the pole.

TIP # 8.
Make your first shot count

Similar to Tip #7, making your first shot count seems like a no-brainer. As hundreds of frustrated deer hunters can attest as they fruitlessly empty their clips at a fleeing trophy every opening morning, it just isn't necessarily so. After sitting for several hours, it is easy to rush your shot when deer arrive in your hunting area.

Move slowly, get a good steady rest and drill the deer with your first shot. If you miss that initial opportunity, you will almost always be shooting at a running, bounding whitetail and go home without venison.

Members admire buck shot by Kurt Kraft in 1998.

The woods yearly ring on opening day with the echoes of multiple shots fired (and missed) by inexperienced hunters who rushed their first, best shot at a nice buck.

Hitting a running deer is difficult, even for the most skillful hunter. Don't fool yourself! Your best shot is almost always your first one. Make it count and you will be eating venison!

Blow the first shot and you will be babbling to yourself as to what you should have done.

Most hunters at the Pine Hill Club make good on their first shot.

Obviously, the buck pole, as shown in the pictures included in this book, speaks for itself and reflects the hunting skills of the members.

We have never failed to hang multiple bucks at the Pine Hill Club deer camp. Making certain of our first shot helps guarantee the pole will be straining under the weight of heavy bucks.

TIP # 9.
Don't charge out of your blind immediately after you shoot the deer

Many hunters, after shooting at a deer, immediately rush to the spot of the shot. This is not the behavior of a veteran hunter!

After shooting at a deer, chamber another shell, watch the reaction of the deer, and visually mark the escape route, if the deer runs. Obviously, if you miss the first shot, keep shooting as long as you have a chance of bagging the animal

If the deer drops in its tracks, be ready for a second shot. It is not uncommon for a wounded deer to get up and run off after being knocked down. Always be ready for a second shot and stay in your blind.

I made such a mistake in 1985. My "greenhorn" reaction still haunts me as an experienced deer hunter.

A beautiful eight-point buck was leading a pack of does directly toward my stand. His horns glistened in the morning light. I waited until he was within 40 yards of my stand, took careful aim and fired. The buck dropped immediately!

Instead of watching him on the ground, I jumped up and quickly approached the downed deer.

When I approached within 20 feet of the buck, he suddenly jumped to his feet and bolted toward the heavy cedar swamp. Rapidly I fired twice, but never touched the fleeing trophy.

Frustrated by my actions, I checked for blood sign. Finding limited blood, I decided to give the deer an hour's reprieve before I began the track.

After the hour had elapsed, I tracked the buck for a quarter mile; finding only a sparse blood trail. Finally the buck crossed a road, leaving our camp property. While standing and pondering what I should do, I heard a single shot from the direction of the wounded deer.

The next day I heard my neighbor had killed a beautiful eight-point buck at the same time that I had heard the shot.

I will never forget this mistake! It was a hard lesson for a veteran deer hunter.

Don't charge out of your blind immediately after taking a shot. Be ready to take a second, well-aimed shot, if needed. The odds are in your favor if you stay put for a few minutes after your first shot. When they're dead, they're dead for a long time.

TIP # 10.
Never look for the whole deer

Deer are masters of camouflage and concealment. They instinctively put brush, trees or cover between you and them.

Successful hunters learn to look for slight movements in a seemingly motionless forest. This movement might be a quick flick of a tail, ghost-like body movement, the tilt of "Mickey Mouse" ears as the deer checks for danger, or a glint of sunlight off a polished antler.

Hunters rarely see a whole deer at initial sighting. Oftentimes, tiny movements, like those noted, materialize into a mature buck sneaking through the forest.

Always watch for any motion in the woods. While it could be a bird or a squirrel, it just might be a trophy buck. Never look for a whole deer!

TIP # 11.
Good optics are essential

Hunting in early morning light or at dusk challenges the sharpest 20-20 vision. Modern optics often make the difference between a success-ful hunt or an empty buck pole.

Disdaining open sights for this reason, I hunt with a variable power scope and a small pair of quality binoculars, usually eight power, to sup-plement my natural vision. A scope of 2-7 or 3-9 power will be most ade-quate for deer hunting.

As a side note, I don't like see-through mounts. They often force the hunter to lift his head to accurately sight. When the hunter lifts his head, even though it is only three-quarters of an inch, this limited movement can and does decrease accuracy.

TIP # 12.
Limit your ammunition

I always put one extra shell in my shirt pocket for emergency use. I carry my other ammunition in a small shell pouch on my belt. Many good quality shell pouches are available at discount and sporting goods stores.

Most guns carry four or five shells, with some lever actions holding up to seven shells. You can always carry extra rounds in your daypack if you desire.

Too many extra shells tend to rattle and make noise. Minimize this noise by carrying only a few extra rounds in a pouch or daypack.

If you need more than ten shells, you have had far more misses than you deserve.

TIP # 13.
Camouflage yourself

As described in Tip # 6, deer are very sensitive to motion or to unusual objects in their environment. Even though I hunt in an enclosed blind, I always use a backdrop or camo-cloth on my back window to prevent the deer from seeing my silhouette in the blind or tree stand.

This allows you to move slightly and not have the deer see you or detect your motion, as easily as they might otherwise. Oak limbs with leaves attached can be placed around your stand as a natural camouflage which can also help prevent the deer from silhouetting you in your stand.

TIP # 14.
Carry a small knife and keep it sharp

A good knife is second in importance only to your rifle as a critical tool for deer hunting.

I prefer a folding knife, with a short, three to three-and-one-half inch lock blade. The Buck 110 hunter is a good choice. A smaller knife, such as this, is more than adequate to field dress deer, is lightweight, and is easy to carry.

Novice hunters often sport eight-to-ten inch, Jim Bowie-type knives. Unless they plan on hand-to-hand combat with a grizzly bear, such unwieldy burdens are unnecessary. Leave these movie knives in the camp. You can always chop onions with them when preparing supper.

A sharp knife allows you to make proper cuts on the deer and prevents you from struggling to cut through the chest cavity. We have all heard the old folk saying that more people are cut by dull knives than sharp ones. I believe it. I always sharpen my knife before going into the woods. You should do the same.

Geoff Quick and eight pointer shot opening day in 2000.

I don't like to keep my knife on my belt. This helps me avoid catching a belted knife on my chair or hitting it on the walls of the blind.

Generally, I keep my knife secured in my daypack. After you have killed your buck, you will have lots of time to secure your knife to field dress the animal.

TIP # 15.

Remove your rifle sling when sitting in a blind

Hunters using a blind should always remove their rifle sling after they enter the structure. Slings swing, move and catch on objects contained in a hunting stand.

In addition to unwanted motion, the sling may get in the way of your shot. I use my rifle sling to carry the weapon to and from the blind and as an emergency drag rope. Otherwise, I remove it and store it out of the way in my blind. Most blinds offer a good rest for shooting and hunters don't need the encumbering sling to help stabilize their shot.

TIP # 16.

Keep your rifle in a ready position

Hunters should always keep their rifle within easy reach. I prefer to keep my rifle on my lap in the prime early morning and late evening hours. If you have to leave your blind to answer nature's call, take your rifle along with you.

When you sight a deer, you want the rifle available to scope the deer, not leaning it in a corner of the blind. Having it immediately at hand provides you with a quick, ready-aim-shoot option. As always, never take the safety off unless you have spotted game that you plan to shoot.

TIP # 17.
Look for evidence that you have hit the deer

After taking a shot, carefully observe the reaction of the deer to your shot. Whitetails will normally provide you with visual evidence of a hit. Note exactly what happened when you fired your rifle.

"Did the deer hunch?"

"Did the deer fall?"

"Did the deer whirl and run?"

"Did the deer drop its tail?"

If you cannot immediately find blood or other evidence of a good hit, get off the track. Go back to your stand, sit down and rethink your shot.

If you push a wounded deer, you may jump the animal. Adrenaline takes over and the deer might run long distances. If left alone, a fatally hit deer will often lie down and die, not too far from where he was first shot.

One of the biggest mistakes a novice hunter makes is to push the animal too quickly after a shot and get a wounded deer back on its feet and running. Wait! Get help from fellow hunters in your party to look for the trail if you're convinced you hit the deer.

TIP # 18.
Carry a short rope to your deer stand

For reasons unknown to me, many a hunter leaves camp without a dragging rope. If you shoot a deer, without having a rope along, you will discover one of huntings greatest physical challenges. Dragging a large, whitetail buck through the woods without a rope is a daunting task at best.

In such a case, your rifle sling might be used or the antlers can provide good handles for dragging. However, believe me, a dragging rope makes your task much easier. It also allows you to easily hang the deer for cooling and draining once you reach camp.

For this reason alone, I always include a twelve-foot piece of rope in my backpack for dragging a deer.

A rope can be handy in other ways also. For instance, twice on hunts near Michigan's Tobacco River, I have had to drag a dead deer, which tried to ford the stream after being shot, from watery brush piles. Pulling the heavy animal out of such a tangle would have been extremely difficult without the help of a rope.

TIP # 19.
Take marking tape to your deer stand

Many hunters use a handkerchief, shirt, hat or other clothing to mark the trail of a wounded deer. However, carrying orange marking tape is a better idea, easier on your clothes, and takes up very little space in your daypack.

Personally, I prefer the orange rolls of marking tape that surveyors use. It is inexpensive, easily packed, and you can spot the marker in heavy timber or thick brush.

This makes establishing a track line and marking last blood a much simpler task for the hunter and trackers.

TIP # 20.
Do only a preliminary field dressing in the woods

I never try to split the pelvic bone of a deer in the field. Without the assistance of a saw or hatchet, which I don't normally pack into my blind, this is a most difficult and unnecessary chore in the woods. You can always complete cleaning the deer in camp, when it is hanging on the buck pole and you have the help from other camp members.

In the woods you should get the lungs, stomach and intestines out and let the deer drain. Wash the body cavity out with water from your stand or snow, if available. This process will get easier with time and the number of deer killed. Many veteran hunters can quickly and adequately field dress a deer within five minutes or so.

TIP # 21.
Get to your hunting area before daylight

Successful deer hunters normally arrive at their deer blind before the crack of dawn.

I always get to my blind no less than 45 minutes before daylight.

This quiet time allows me to get mentally and physically prepared for the coming hunt, without feeling rushed.

Use this time to remove your sling and any extra clothing you might have worn into the blind. Secure the sling, clothes, your coffee thermos and any other objects that might make noise at the wrong time.

Over 50 percent of Michigan's bucks are harvested on opening day. Therefore, be prepared for your opportunity when it comes knocking. Successful hunters always arrive at their deer stands well before first light.

TIP # 22.

Take reading material to your blind

I always take reading material to my deer blind. In fact, I usually leave several magazines, one or two novels, and a newspaper in the blind prior to the hunting season.

Reading material allows me to occupy time and helps the long days go faster. Good books, stories or literature can help keep you in your stand longer and increase your chances of waiting out a trophy buck.

TIP # 23.

Always eat a good breakfast before going hunting

Remaining in a deer stand for twelve consecutive hours requires skill and patience. For me, having a full stomach is important and allows me to sit in comfort for many of those long hours.

In addition to a filling breakfast, I always take a thermos of hot coffee, several sandwiches and candy bars to the stand for use throughout the day.

TIP # 24.

Pack a survival kit

Mother Nature has a mysterious way of getting your attention when you are deer hunting.

For instance, without toilet paper, you are always in an awkward position to respond to nature's call.

My daypack regularly contains a survival kit of matches, a compass, toilet paper, water bottle, cough drops, anti-acid, band aids and chewing gum to cover any emergency that may occur.

TIP # 25.

Be sure your chair doesn't make noise

Many hunters have missed a chance for a trophy buck because of a squeaky chair in their blind. As noted in Tip # 5, silence is golden.

Be quiet in your blind and be certain your chair doesn't make noise. Chairs should be quiet, comfortable and provide you with noise-free movement. This may sound simple, but many a buck has escaped thanks to an inopportune squeak! Attend to errant squeaks with WD40 well in advance of opening day in order to avoid fresh oil smells.

TIP # 26.

Never take your billfold to your hunting stand

I always leave my billfold in a secure place in my truck or at the cabin. If you walk through heavy brush or thicket, you can easily lose your billfold. This is especially true if you have to remove clothing to answer nature's call or to gut a deer.

You don't need your billfold while in the woods. They're hard to find in the snow and woods. Leave it in a safe, secure place.

TIP # 27.

Always take your hunting license and deer tag

Nothing is more embarrassing than shooting a deer and discovering you cannot tag the animal because your tag is back at camp. I either pin my tag INSIDE my shirt or place it in a secure, buttoned shirt pocket.

This way the tag cannot catch on branches and is always ready when needed.

Additionally, if the Conservation Officer stops you to check your hunting license, you can easily access both your hunting license and deer tag.

TIP # 28.

Take a watch with you

When I sit in my deer stand, I like to note the time I spotted deer for future reference. A watch also allows you to gauge the amount of time left before darkness arrives and lets you note the time you shot your buck.

I prefer the Indiglo variety of watches. The soft light in the watch allows you to not only clearly read the time, but also serves as a mini-flashlight in the pitch darkness of your predawn blind

TIP # 29.
Take a small flashlight

Few things are more frustrating than discovering you have forgotten to pack a flashlight in your stand. Hiking through the woods in the cloudy, rainy darkness without a light makes it extremely difficult to locate your blind. Returning to camp in the dark can be equally frustrating.

After years of deer hunting, I usually place a spare flashlight in my daypack in case I break a bulb, run out of battery power, or need a back up to my regular flashlight.

Personally, I prefer a mini-mag type of light you can hold between your teeth. This allows you to use both hands, if necessary. I have gutted many deer with this small light held between my teeth.

TIP # 30.
Use oak and pine branches when making a natural blind

When making a deer blind from natural materials, whether a tree or ground stand, the use of heavily leafed oak limbs and thickly needled pine branches make a great combination. The oak leaves provide good break-up cover and will remain on the limbs longer than those of almost any other type of tree. The pine branches and needles not only supply a long-lasting camouflage, but also provide a natural cover scent for the hunter.

TIP # 31.
Be especially alert in the morning and evening

Most big bucks travel during the early morning light or the dim light of dusk. You may see trophy bucks at any time of the day, but dawn and dusk are the critically important hours when most hunters fill their tags. Always be on high alert during these times when hunting deer.

TIP # 32.
Spend time in your stand before season

I always like to spend time in my deer stand prior to the hunting season. This ties in with scouting the area around the stand. Spending time in the blind before season allows me to observe deer travelling in the area and to note which direction, they are moving. On many occasions, I have spotted a good buck prior to the hunting season.

This practice increases your chances on opening day and gives you a challenge to think about prior to season. Many successful deer hunters I know spend time in their hunting stand prior to the season.

Note: If you bow hunt your rifle area, you will be able to note deer movement and direction. This knowledge of deer movement can greatly help you in rifle season.

TIP # 33.
Stock your blind in advance
Smart deer hunters adhere to the Boy Scout Motto — Be Prepared!

By stocking your blind prior to opening day, you don't have to carry any extra weight through the brush as you walk to your hunting spot. In addition you can inventory the items at your leisure prior to season and use a checklist to avoid forgetting critical gear.

As noted earlier, I always stock my blind with toilet paper, paper towels, candy, soda and bottled water prior to the hunt. In addition to these materials, I add several good books or magazines to occupy the long hours spent watching and waiting for a big whitetail buck.

TIP # 34.
Keep the floor of the blind clear of noisy items
Whether you hunt in a man-made, commercial type of stand or in a natural blind, the floor/ground should be kept free from candy wrappers, dry leaves or other items that may rattle and scare off the deer.

One of the first things I do when arriving at my hunting blind is check the floor for any possible noisy items. One snap from a dry leaf or carelessly discarded candy wrapper will usually spook any wary deer nearby.

TIP # 35.
Check your ammunition prior to hunting
If you buy new ammunition for the upcoming deer season, be certain to shoot a few rounds in your hunting rifle when you are sighting

in. Although ammunition makers strive for uniformity in their loads, I believe time and conditions sometimes can make a difference in the point of impact of a bullet, even from the same gun. Always test fire your ammunition prior to using it in the field.

TIP # 36.
Use 'bright eyes' to map the path to your blind
Although you wish to enter your blind with as little noise, fuss and light as possible, a commercially available, reflective thumbtack, such as "Bright Eyes", can be used to mark your path to your stand.

The reflective thumbtacks allow you to stay on the trail without getting lost and stumbling through the woods in search of your blind. They last for years and provide unobtrusive, helpful markers to and from your hunting stand especially when trying to find your stand in the darkness of a cloudy, windy, rainy predawn hunt.

TIP # 37.
Process your own deer
By skinning and cutting up your own deer, you increase the pleasure of the hunt. In addition, you know how your meat is cut and know that you are getting your own venison.

True or false, we have all heard horror stories about meat-processing plants. Most of these butchers are very pro-

Bruce Anderson and Rick Mills with a buck harvested in 1999.

fessional and do a quality job. However, to avoid any questions of cleanliness or of getting the wrong meat, I always skin, cut and wrap my own deer. This also allows me to make the cuts our family enjoys.

There are a number of publications available that describe this process. It is not difficult, especially after you do it the first time.

TIP # 38.
Use a range finder to mark shooting distances

When hunting the same area year after year, you should mark the distance of your potential shots with a range finder. This information allows you to know if you have a 50-yard shot or a 200-yard shot. I like to mark my shooting lanes with a range finder prior to season. This information increases my accuracy by allowing me to adjust my sight to compensate for known distances when a trophy buck appears in one of my shooting lanes.

TIP # 39.
Give yourself enough space in your stand

Hunters who are tightly confined in their shooting space because they constructed their blind too small reduce their chances for a successful shot. I always build our Pine Hill Club stands a minimum of five feet in all directions. Stands that are four-feet by four-feet, a common pattern, are cramped, in my opinion.

These small structures are mistakes waiting to happen when you bump your rifle on a ledge, wall or some other object in the blind. The same is true for natural stands. Build your stand large enough for comfort, as well as concealment. Allow yourself room to quietly and comfortably move in your enclosure.

TIP # 40.
Use a face mask in cold weather

Few things are worst than shivering in a cold stand throughout a long day of hunting in the woods. If you have a freezing wind in your face, as often happens in Michigan during deer season, you will be cold and uncomfortable if you don't take advantage of as much protection as you can.

I always use a full-face mask when hunting in cold conditions. The mask protects my face and prevents potential frostbite. Besides, being warm allows hunters to sit quietly for longer periods of time than they could otherwise. It also adds to your personal well being in your stand. Finally, a face mask provides a hunter with the additional advantage of camouflaging his face, which often can otherwise serve as a neon-like warning sign to wary whitetails.

TIP # 41.

Use a decoy to attract deer

Decoys are the ultimate lure. In the rut, a buck's mind is on romance. He is seeking a doe in heat or a rival buck to fight. Use the decoy to take advantage of this fact of nature.

Bow hunting over a deer decoy can be a very effective ploy, especially when using a rattle call. Decoys are not normally recommended for use during rifle season, especially on public hunting land.

Using a decoy, doe-in-heat lure, and rattling can help you bag your buck.

TIP # 42.

Watch the does and fawns

Hunters who study the reaction of does and fawns have natural watchdogs working for them in the woods.

I once shot a beautiful six-point buck that was pointed out to me by a watchful doe.

The hearing and eyesight of one deer can tip you off to other animals approaching. Successful hunters watch carefully the actions of does and fawns.

Many times I have observed does and fawns snap their heads up and focus on approaching game. It may be a signal of a squirrel or turkey nearby, but oftentimes it can mean a trophy buck is sneaking through the woods! If you are prepared when a big buck comes by your stand, your chances of successfully harvesting him increase dramatically.

TIP # 43.

Use your ears to locate deer

Deer, while quiet, are not soundless ghosts in the forest. Hunters oftentimes can hear deer approaching before the animals are spotted. This is especially true in thick brush, on frozen ground, or when the ground is covered with dry leaves.

The snap of a twig, the slow, gentle rustling of leaves, or the snort of a deer winding you can often be heard long before you see the game.

By listening carefully, you can often detect an approaching deer before you see the quarry. Your ears are a valued asset that can significantly improve your chances of success.

TIP # 44.
Record time and sighting of deer

Successful hunters keep a mental or written log of the time, location and number of deer sighted during each day's hunt.

A creature of habit, whitetails normally feed at specific times or move to their bedding areas in a regular pattern.

By recording the number of deer, types, locations and times of sightings you can enhance your chances for future success.

Frequently, if undisturbed, you see the same animals in the same general area at approximately the same time.

This information may enable you to set up an ambush and put venison on the table.

TIP # 45.
Check wind direction regularly

Hunters who fail to observe changing wind direction are at a distinct disadvantage when hunting whitetail deer.

Neighbor Gary Tilmann displays a nice ten pointer shot late in season.

As noted earlier, deer have a tremendous ability to detect human odor. In addition to using a commercial scent cover, as advised, always hunt into the wind.

Changing wind direction may require you to change hunting tactics.

At the Pine Hill Club I always check the wind direction before heading into the woods. With multiple blinds to choose from, I always use a blind that utilizes wind direction to keep my scent from blowing to the primary runways. Additionally, I often tie a short piece of orange surveyor's tape to a limb. The tape then serves as an immediate and very visible wind indicator.

Hunters who are observant of wind direction put more venison on the table. Enough said!

TIP # 46.
Keep duct tape in your duffel bag

Many emergency situations occur in the woods that require you to make immediate, though temporary, repairs. Duct tape will often do the job.

I have used duct tape to bandage a cut finger, repair a broken sling, fix eye glasses that lost a screw, repair a broken window and patch hip boots.

With duct tape and WD 40 you can handle almost any situation. If it moves and it shouldn't, tape it! If it doesn't move and it should, spray it. Do these tasks well in advance of the opener to eliminate fresh oil smells!

Though temporary, duct tape repairs have allowed me to remain in the woods and continue hunting when I would otherwise have been forced to return to camp to affect repairs.

Frequently, I mark my boots with duct tape to avoid mix-ups in a camp full of hunters.

Duct tape and WD40, although not permanent, will serve the serious hunter well.

TIP # 47.
Use odor-absorbing powder on rubber boots

Hunters wearing ankle-fitting rubber boots often experience difficulty getting them on in the morning.

Rubber boots tend to retain moisture from your feet and can become clammy if not adequately dried.

A small sprinkle of odor-absorbing powder helps you slide your feet into the boot and reduces body odor.

TIP # 48.
Store hunting clothes in pine/cedar boughs

Nothing can ruin a hunter's chances for a trophy buck faster than having the buck detect his scent.

Storing hunting clothes in a plastic bag containing pine or cedar boughs greatly reduces human odor.

I have used this natural odor-camouflaging technique for years and strongly believe in the odor-reducing value of this coniferous foliage.

Tip # 49.
Regularly check blind propane levels

Little is more frustrating than having a blind's heater quit on a cold, frigid morning because you didn't have enough fuel to get you through the day.

You can avoid this by either leaving an extra tank of propane outside your blind or more simply by regularly checking the propane level in your cylinder.

In a similar line, before beginning tracks, after dark, I always check the propane level in the Coleman lanterns.

Being in a pitch black cedar swamp, without light, is not a pleasant experience! Neither is shivering uncomfortably in a cold stand.

TIP # 50.
Use a black marker to label your personal equipment

Most deer camps are havens of activity with hats, gun cases, boxes of similar shells, knives and flashlights stored indiscriminately throughout the cabin. As Uncle Vern could attest, equipment mix-up is a common place risk in such an environment.

Therefore, I always label my personal equipment with a permanent marker.

This simple process helps avoid confusion of ownership and allows you to use your own equipment. If you don't think this is important, think about picking up a box of .270 shells for your 30-06 and not discovering the error until you're in your blind and dawn is breaking.

Avoid this camp hassle by urging hunters to mark their personal equipment.

Marking also helps to identify the owners of any items inevitably left in camp.

In summary we all need all the help we can get to consistently succeed in putting fresh venison on the table. Hunters who follow these fifty tips for success while deer hunting will put more venison on the pole.

These suggestions, while not all-inclusive, will clearly allow you to more successfully pit your skill as a hunter against the master of the woods, the whitetail deer.

All these tips are used at the Pine Hill Club and have been proven in the field. They will work for the conscientious hunter.

Be prepared for the challenge and increase your odds of bagging your big buck!

GOOD HUNTING!

Buck shot by Rick Mills – displayed on wall of cabin.

CHAPTER 9

Deer Blind Construction (Rifle/Bow)

ost private Michigan deer camps have permanent hunting blinds to accommodate the hunter's need for shelter, concealment and comfort. Common names for these structures include: blinds, posts, and stands. Terminology varies with geographic location throughout the state.

Hunters located in the Upper Peninsula of Michigan call their hunting structures "posts." Hunters situated in the Lower Peninsula of our northern state term their structures "stands" or more commonly "blinds." Whatever term is used, the purposes are always the same: shelter, comfort and concealment.

Many private camp members challenge each other's talent and creativity in constructing and locating their hunting structures. Some hunters revel in the elegance built into their miniature homes in the woods.

My standards are simple, when it comes to the constructing such a structure. Requirements always include concealment, good vision throughout the surrounding area, warmth, protection from the elements, and quiet.

Throughout many years of owning a deer camp I have experimented with many types of hunting structures. Currently, I am convinced the plans contained in this chapter reflect among the best overall blind designs, resulting from years of trial and error in construction.

As with the "best" deer rifle, equipment and knife, hunters can argue for hours about the best hunting blind. Given that fact of hunting camp, the designs shared here work well for us and they should do the same for you.

Properly constructed hunting stands should allow a hunter to sit for long hours in comfort near proven deer runways. These small buildings must provide shelter from the wind, cold and snow that normally accompany deer season.

Our first hunting blinds at the Pine Hill Club were constructed from logs and brush found in the woods. These simple, make-shift structures offered limited camouflage cover for the hunter, but no shelter from the rain or wet snow that commonly occur in the mid-November hunting season.

Most hunters in our early years used a coffee can filled with charcoal briquettes for heat. A tin can, filled with toilet paper soaked in rubbing alcohol, also served as a smelly source of warmth for their hands and feet.

Holes were punched in the bottom of the coffee cans to provide for airflow. Ventilation was not a problem, as the hunters sat in the open surrounded by brush walls.

No roofs were used in these early, temporary, makeshift blinds.

Plastic, five-gallon pails often provided a seat. A thermos of hot coffee, lunch, flashlight and a rope were all transported to the blind in a small backpack. Most hunters carried extra socks and gloves to replace those that often became wet due to either rain or snow.

Currently at the Pine Hill Club we have thirty permanent hunting blinds. With 760 acres available to hunt, we have ample room to construct and safely locate these structures.

I should also note the hunters in the blinds at our deer camp usually see multiple deer throughout each day. Some of these blinds are located in dense cedar swamp, while others are positioned on open oak ridges. Several blinds are positioned along the edge of farm fields covered with grasses.

Author next to his hunting blind named the "Chapel".

As with the variety of locations, the shooting opportunities vary widely. Some blinds, such as those in the swamps, only allow for fairly close shots. Others located near alfalfa fields allow hunters the potential of shots up to 250-400 yards.

The majority of these hunting blinds are five-by-six foot in size. All are constructed from wood, painted black, and have window openings located 41 inches from the floor. The window openings are 9 inches in height and have folding glass windows (Windows fold up.) Small hinges and screen-door fasteners secure the windows when the blind is not in use.

Blinds have carpeting on the floor to reduce noise and use a small, propane, Nu-Way Stove for heat. A 20-pound propane cylinder is placed on the outside wall of the blind, with a valve and hose connecting the propane to the stove. The stoves also serve to heat coffee and soup for hungry hunters during the long hours in the woods.

The Nu-Way Stoves have an oxygen sensor to provide further safety for the hunter and have served us well over the years. Hunters should always keep a window open for safety's sake when using any stove in an enclosed blind.

Based on an idea gleaned from some UP deer-hunting friends, many of the Pine Hill Club blinds also feature a small shelf that runs under a window on one side of the blind. This allows the hunter to place binoculars, a rifle, and/or a coffee cup in a convenient location. These shelves are also carpeted to minimize noise.

Our blinds are constructed from pressed board (7/16" OSB). They are assembled in six sections: four walls, a floor and a roof. The roof has an overhang of approximately twelve inches to keep the rain from falling directly into the hunting area. A metal drip edge is used to protect the boards on the roof.

Most blinds are situated and leveled on cement blocks. Although Michigan law allows for elevated rifle blinds, only two of the Pine Hill Club blinds are so designed. These blinds are erected approximately five feet in the air. Four-by-six-inch posts are cemented into the ground for support.

These blinds can be easily moved by disassembling them into their six basic parts and transporting them to a different location.

Most of our blinds have been in the same spot for many years, with several being constructed over 25 years ago. (I hunt from a blind constructed in 1975. With minimal maintenance, it remains as good as new.)

Some blinds are moved, however, as we constantly seek to improve hunting opportunities through increased knowledge of the habitat. Sometimes shooting lanes fill in with brush, trees fall into critical shooting areas or other valid reasons will require relocating a blind.

Every blind has a swivel chair and a small table where the hunter can place his daypack, coffee cup or magazines. All blinds have a tin canister to store and protect both food stuffs and emergency toilet articles. Additionally, most of our hunters place a gallon jug of water in their blinds to help wash out a deer cavity and to clean their hands after field dressing a deer.

Needless to say, such a sheltered hunting arrangement is comfortable and provides excellent protection from the elements. All Pine Hill Club hunters have one blind assigned to them for opening day. However, because we have multiple blinds, each may choose from several available hunting locations throughout the season.

We have more blinds than we do members. Normally, non-member guests may not hunt on opening day. With thirty blinds and twenty-one hunters, we have a minimum of nine open spots that are not hunted on any given day.

Blind construction is usually a club workday project for the members. All share in hauling newly constructed blinds to pre-selected locations on camp workdays.

Painting the blinds is also an annual affair. Approximately five blinds are painted each year on a rotation or need basis.

Dave Mills constructing a new blind.

Plans, including a list of materials for construction, are included in this chapter. Prices will vary according to the market at the time and adjustments in size or choice of materials can be made for personal reasons.

As noted, I like a blind that is a minimum of five-by-six foot in dimension, as it allows two people to comfortably sit together and watch for deer. I frequently take one of my grandsons with me while hunting. Occasionally, a close family or camp friend will express a desire to participate in a deer hunt as an observer. The larger blinds allow us to sit together for long periods of time in a warm, secure, and quiet atmosphere.

Many deer camps build hunting blinds four-by-four foot in construction. These stands, I content, are too small. They do not allow hunters the necessary freedom of movement or comfort needed for the long hours of hunting in the woods. Such a small blind increases the difficulty of avoiding noises generated by knocking a gun on the wall or bumping the sides of the stand. A foot added to the size of the blind makes for a much more comfortable unit at a minimal increase in construction cost.

Constructing a deer blind from the plans in this chapter should take approximately ten hours. Many hands can make the work easier and quicker. Each section should be constructed separately, before transporting the disassembled unit to the field. Double-check your work by assembling the blind at the construction site. (At the Pine Hill Club, we build the hunting blinds in a large barn located on the property).

The various sections can then be nailed or screwed together in the field and a final coat of paint added after the blind components have been placed on location. Screwing the sections of the blinds together does allow you to more easily disassemble them if they must be moved at a future date.

All blinds on the Pine Hill Club are named with a sign attached. Referring to the blinds by name helps members know where each other is hunting on any given day.

The "Chapel", "Oak Tree", "Birchwood", "Wigwam", "Four-Korners", "Bog", "Buckhorn", "Iron-Sides", "Swamp Island", "Butcher Shop", "Bear Tooth", "Well-Head", and "Ambush" are but a few of the names of our hunting blinds.

Pine Hill Club members, after thirty years of designing and re-designing deer blinds, have developed the following construction plans:

Rifle — Deer Blind Construction Plans/Diagram at end of chapter

Bow hunting

Only ten or twelve of our camp members are archers. Those who hunt with a bow and arrow are very serious about their deer hunting. All hunt from elevated tree stands.

My concern for safety is noted in the construction of a bow stand.

Many manufacturers today market excellent portable tree stands for the serious archer.

Only three of our members use portable tree stands. The reference section of this book lists several sources for portable tree stands. Most of our hunters use bow stands that are permanently constructed on our property.

On a very personal level, being afraid of heights and concerned about my safety, I never use a portable tree stand. I am simply not comfortable with them.

My preference is a well-constructed, spacious tree stand that provides safety, ease of access and concealment from the elements. We have fourteen permanent tree stands at the Pine Hill Club. All are safe, easily accessed and camouflaged to provide concealment for the hunter. Although we rarely bow hunt in inclement weather, most have roofs that protect the hunter from the rain and snow that occurs during the fall hunting season.

Plans are identified for construction of these permanent tree stands. Again, I note that you must have private land to construct a permanent tree stand.

As with the rifle stand, prices will vary depending on materials selected, market prices and the size of the stand being built. Stand construction will also be impacted by the available tree formations where the stand is to be built.

I prefer a bow stand of approximately four feet by four feet in size with a guardrail to help prevent the hunter from falling from the stand.

Hunters who seek deer with a bow and arrow tend to be passionate about the sport.

Accepting the challenge of seeking a trophy whitetail with this equipment can stretch the maximum limits of the most ardent hunter. Using a "stick and string" to bag venison is the ultimate challenge for any deer hunter.

Bow hunters at our camp are masters of camouflage, the use of scent cover and the great art of patience. Most of the archers are also master trackers of wounded game.

Roger Dixon, a retired superintendent of a county school district, and our second son David, a high school teacher and wrestling coach, spend many hours scouting their hunt areas prior to the October 1st opener. Usually Roger and Dave have spotted a good buck before season begins and spend countless hours deciding how to outsmart the wary whitetail.

Serious bow hunters practice daily to gain proficiency in shooting accurately. We have a target range at the camp and most bow hunters check their sights and tune their shooting skills on a regular basis as they work to increase their accuracy in the field.

Veteran bow hunters use several tree stands so as not to scent up any one area. By rotating between several stands, alternate-hunting locations can settle down if an area has been disturbed by human scent. Deer will quickly return to their normal movement pattern. By using several stands, a bow hunter can also adjust for changing wind direction that might carry his or her scent to the wary deer.

Many manufacturers make quality archery equipment, including portable tree stands.

I will not present a listing of these, due to my lack of familiarity with them. I would recommend that if you would like to use a portable stand, you should check with other bow hunters actually familiar with them.

I have, however, included some basic plans for the construction of permanent bow stands for your use on private property. Always check the game laws regarding construction of permanent structures in your hunting area.

Bow stand situated in large oak tree.

Properly constructed rifle and bow stands will serve the hunter on private property for many years. As with all such structures, proper maintenance is required to keep the wood preserved, windows clear, and ladders solid.

At the Pine Hill Club, we annually inspect all our hunting blinds to be certain they are solid and in good repair. Hunters report any broken steps, rotted wood or cracked windows. Camp maintenance is a constant, but necessary, element of operating a quality hunting property.

Joe Mills beside his blind named "Oak Tree".

Rifle Blind Construction Plans (see rifle blind diagram)

Materials List: 5 ft. X 6 ft. blind

- Seven sheets $7/16$ inch press board OSB – 4ft X 8ft
- One sheet of $7/16$ inch press board OSB – 4ft X 8ft (floor)
- One piece of 1" X I0" pine board – 16 feet long
- One piece of 1" X 10" pine board – 14 feet long
- One roll of roofing (black) 100 square feet
- Four pieces of drip edge – 10 feet long
- Ten pieces of 2" X 4" – 12 feet long
- Fourteen pieces of 2" X 4" – 10 feet long
- Three – 3-inch strap hinges for door
- One hasp lock or other closing devise for door
- Five pounds of 16 common nails (spikes)
- Five pounds of box 7 nails
- One gallon of black latex flat paint and roller

FLOOR PLANS:

- Two pieces of 2" X 4" cut 72" long (floor sides)
- Seven pieces of 2" X 4" cut 57 inches long (floor joists)
- Place floor joists – 12" on center

FRONT SIDE:

- Two pieces of 2" X 4" cut 75 inches long with one inch drop at back
- Four pieces of 2" X 4" cut 69 inches long for cross pieces
- Cross piece is placed at top, bottom and measured 4I" and 50" from base

BACK SIDE:

- Two pieces of 2" X 4" cut 69 inches long with one inch drop at back
- Three pieces of 2" X 4" cut 69 inches long for cross pieces
- Cross piece is placed at top, bottom and 50" from base
- Four pieces of 2" X 4" cut 48 inches long for door frame (note drawing)

SIDE PLANS (make two sides)

- Two pieces 2" X 4" cut 74 inches
- Two pieces 2" X 4" cut 69 inches

- Eight pieces 2" X 4" cut 50 inches for cross pieces (see diagram)
- Cross piece is placed at top, bottom and measured 4l" and 50" from base
- Be sure that sides are sheeted opposite one another (right and left side)

ROOF PLANS:
- Two pieces 2" X 4" cut 64 ½ inches for side pieces
- Six pieces 2" X 4" cut 49 inches for roof joist
- Two sheets of $^{7}/_{126}$ inch pressboard for roof
- You will have a 1'5" overhang – all the way around frame
- Nail a 1" X 10" piece of pine board along edge to support drip edge
- When nailed with #7 commons the roof will set on top of blind

DOOR PLANS:
- Two pieces 2" X 4" cut 48 inches long (notch corners to lay cross piece on top & bottom)
- Two pieces 2" X 4" cut 27 inches long for door (door opening is 30 inches wide)
- One piece 2" X 4" cut 23 inches long for cross piece (see diagram)
- Notch corners 1 ½ inches by 3 ½ inches (see diagram)
- Place 23 inch cross piece at 4l inches from base of door (see diagram)
- Place screen door hook to hold shut from inside
- Attach hinges to secure door to blind
- Sheet door with 7 $^{1}/_{16}$ inch OSB
- Cut out window opening (I prefer a 9 inch opening)

WINDOW PLANS:
- One sheet ¾ inch plywood – good one side
- Two tubes Dupont silicone – clear
- Two – 2" inch strap hinges (two per window)
- Two – small screen door hooks (butterfly type to close windows)
- Cut plywood into 12-inch strips. This will cover the 9-inch window opening
- Using a skill saw and jig saw – cut a 6-inch high opening for each window leaving 3 inches on top and each side
- Buy glass cut that is 8 inches high by length of your window. (allow for a one inch lap on each side and a one inch lap from top to bottom)
- Using silicone adhesive to attach glass to window frame

- Using strap hinges – attach windows from top so they swing upward
- Using butterfly closures – secure windows from bottom (note: you will need a short piece of 2" X 4" nailed below window joist and a short piece of ¾ inch cut 6 inches long by 2 inches to secure window from bottom)

Bow Stand Plans* (see bow stand diagram)

*Use treated pine for all bow stand construction or rough sawn oak boards

Materials List: (4ft. X 4 ft. Bow stand)

LADDER

- Two 16 foot 2" X 4" in pine (for ladder)
- Four – ten foot 2" X 4" in pine for steps
- You will need fourteen pieces of 2" X 4" cut 24 inches in length for steps

RAILS for SIDE-WALLS

- Twelve – eight foot 2" X 4" for rails

BASE and FLOOR

- Five – eight foot 1" X 6" inch rough sawn oak for base.
- Enough rough sawn oak for floor.
- Treated 2 X 6 pine and regular treated pine deck boards will also work.

ROOF

- Four – eight foot 2" X 4"
- One sheet of ½ inch exterior grade plywood for roof
- Small piece of rolled roofing

HARDWARE

- Five pounds of 16 common spikes
- Five pounds of 4" ring nails (pole barn type)
- Box of 2 inch wood screws
- One gallon of black exterior paint
- One can green camouflage spray paint

BASE OF BOW STAND (14 feet off ground)

- Locate three large trees along good runway
- Using an aluminum ladder, secure oak brace to trees (use level and 5" ring nails)
- Bracing must be level to provide a solid floor for bow stand
- Secure oak cross pieces for floor joists
- Using chain saw – cut joists to fit properly

RAILING FOR SIDES

- Using 2" X 4"s build three side rails that are 36 inches in height.
- Be sure to leave a 30-inch opening to enter blind
- Cut 2" X 4" pieces 33 inches in length for rails (number will vary depending on size of your bow stand)
- Place rails one foot apart and secure top and bottom with 16 common spikes and wood screws
- Add oak or pine branches to provide camouflage for side rails.

Bow stand at edge of cedar swamp.

ROOF (optional)

If you build a roof on your bow stand use 2" X 4" pieces located at least six to seven feet high. (Depending on your bow length and your height you do not want to raise your bow and strike the roof on your bow stand. Vary height accordingly)

Using black and green spray paint, cover your ladder and all exposed pieces of wood. You can use a sheet of plywood or OSB board for your roof. Cover roof with a small piece of rolled roofing to keep out snow and rain

Rifle Blind Construction Diagrams

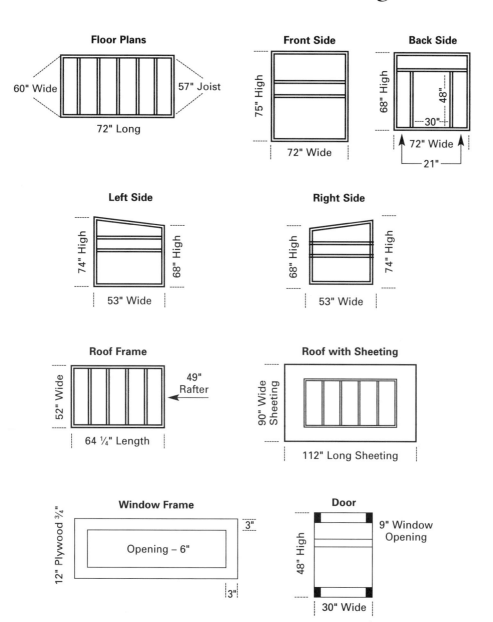

Floor Plans

60" Wide   57" Joist

72" Long

Front Side

75" High

72" Wide

Back Side

68" High

48"

30"

72" Wide

21"

Left Side

74" High   68" High

53" Wide

Right Side

68" High   74" High

53" Wide

Roof Frame

52" Wide

49" Rafter

64 ¼" Length

Roof with Sheeting

90" Wide Sheeting

112" Long Sheeting

Window Frame

12" Plywood ¾"

Opening – 6"

3"

3"

Door

48" High

9" Window Opening

30" Wide

Bow Stand Construction Diagrams

Ladder – 16 Feet in Length

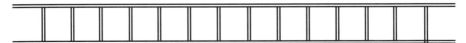

Steps are placed 12" apart using 2" x 4" pieces

Base of Bow Stand

Secure 1" x 6" Oak
on three trees.

Level and ring nail.

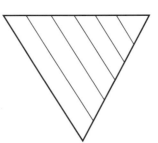

Cut floor joists and
anchor with screws
and nails.

Length of floor joists
will vary depending on
size of base.

Use oak boards to
sheet floor.

Side Rail – Cut to Length

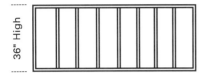

36" High

NOTE: Cut rails to fit bow stand.
Length will vary depending on
size of bow stand.

Entrance Door – Rail

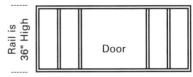

Rail is
36" High

Door

30" Door Opening

CHAPTER 10

Deer Camp Recipes

ating well in a deer camp is as much a part of deer hunting as is the hunting itself. The Pine Hill Club is certainly no exception to this rule.

Abundant food, hearty appetites and good cooking make for a comfortable, pleasant stay in any woods!

This section focuses on popular Pine Hill Club camp recipes we regularly prepare. The recipes shared herein have been proven over time and should delight and satisfy the appetite of the most discriminating hunter. They generally are simple and quick to make in the camp kitchen.

One or two members primarily do the cooking at the Pine Hill Club. They share a common desire for excellent meals and a talent for preparing food. Other members wash dishes and perform clean-up chores, while encouraging and praising the merits of the camp cooks. Not only is the food appetizing, it is filling and satisfying.

Criticizing the camp cook will quickly result in an invitation to prove your own culinary skills.

"If you don't like the food, don't eat it, but keep your mouth shut," is an unwritten rule in most deer camps. Another well-known adage is, "He who criticizes, cooks the next meal!"

It goes without saying that every deer camp should maintain well-stocked shelves of the basic ingredients for preparing camp food. Salt, pepper, chili powder, flour, sugar, butter and cooking oil are all staples for every camp kitchen.

The meals listed below are regularly served at our camp. Members eat well and no person leaves the camp hungry or lighter, unless it is by his own choosing.

In addition to the meals prepared at camp, the wives of many Pine Hill Club hunters like to send a favorite dish to deer camp. Homemade pies, lasagna, soups, brownies, cakes and other special treats often grace our tables. Our spouses always put forth their best efforts for these special treats. Life "in the swamp" is tough, but someone's got to do it!

I hope you gain some ideas from this section on deer camp recipes. ENJOY!

Uncle Vern prepares bacon and eggs for breakfast.

Deer Camp Chili

Ingredients:
- Two or three pounds of ground venison burger
- Two large cans of kidney beans
- Four large cans of tomatoes (two should be diced or whole tomatoes)
- Two large onions

Brown the venison burger in a large skillet in two tablespoons of olive oil.

Sauté the chopped onions in a frying pan with two tablespoons of butter.

Empty the kidney beans and tomatoes into a large pan with a cover.

Add the browned venison, drained, and sautéed onions to this mixture.

Salt and pepper to taste.

Add one tablespoon of chili powder.

Heat slowly for about one hour. Don't boil or overheat this mixture. Stir frequently. Cover pan while heating slowly.

NOTE: Chili gets better with age. The second day this mixture will taste even better. Members who like more chili powder can add their own.

Overall, our camp does not like the chili to have too hot a bite. A cup or two of medium salsa will add significant "kick", if your camp members like spicy chili. You can alter the mixture to meet personal taste.

Liver and Onions

Ingredients:
- One or two large deer livers
- Two or more large onions that are peeled and sliced into small rings
- Olive oil

Slice liver into thin strips approximately one-quarter inch thick.

Place olive oil in frying pan cover and heat. Saute' onions in hot oil until tender.

Add the sliced liver with the onions and cover the pan. Cook slowly.

Serve when liver has been thoroughly cooked and is brown throughout when cut with a knife. A word of caution: Don't overcook the liver. It can quickly turn into "shoe leather".

Serve with rice or potatoes.

Lemon Pepper Venison Steaks

Ingredients:
- Several pounds of venison steaks depending on number of hunters
- Olive oil
- Lemon pepper

Slice steaks approximately three-quarters of an inch thick. As with all venison, trim off fat and gristle.

Place in a large frying pan with olive oil. Heat oil to hot prior to placing the steaks in the pan.

Fry rapidly until the meat is pink in the middle. As with the liver, don't overcook venison steak.
Generously sprinkle lemon pepper on top of steaks when frying. Members may salt and pepper to taste.

Turn steaks once.

Bean Soup

Ingredients:
- Two to four pounds of navy beans
- Large ham bone and 1 pound of chunked ham
- Two cups celery – chopped
- Two cups chopped onions
- One teaspoon salt
- One teaspoon pepper
- One-half teaspoon dried thyme, crushed

Rinse beans with cold water and place in large covered cooking kettle

Add water to cover the beans and boil. Let boiled beans cool for one hour.

Drain and rinse beans.

Add water to cover the beans and place back on stove.

Add ham bone and chunked ham, as well as all remaining chopped onions and other ingredients.

Bring mixture to boil and then reduce heat to slow simmer.

Continue to cook beans at slow heat for approximately two hours.

Check to be sure beans are soft and tender. If not, cook some more. Add water, if necessary.

Salt and pepper to taste and serve with crackers.

Venison Stew

Ingredients:
- Two to four pounds of diced venison steak
- One cup of flour
- One can of tomato juice
- One large can of whole or diced tomatoes
- One pound of green beans
- One pound of canned corn
- One pound of canned potatoes
- One pound of canned carrots
- One large onion sautéed

Roll diced venison in flour and brown in frying pan with olive oil.

Place the tomato juice, whole tomatoes, green beans, corn, carrots and sautéed onion in large kettle with cover.

Bring the ingredients to a slow simmer. Add browned venison and potatoes.

Cook slowly for approximately one hour. Add enough water to be sure all ingredients are covered.

Add salt and pepper to taste and enjoy.

Deer Camp Spaghetti

Ingredients:

- Two pounds of spaghetti
- One quart of spaghetti sauce
- One pound of venison burger
- One can of mushrooms
- One can of tomato soup

Place spaghetti in large pan of boiling water. Cook until tender.

Brown venison burger in frying pan with two tablespoons of olive oil.

Place spaghetti sauce, mushrooms and tomato soup in large saucepan. Heat slowly and stir occasionally.

Add browned venison burger to sauce pan and stir. Don't boil.

When spaghetti is cooked, drain and rinse with cold water.

Serve spaghetti topped with meat-sauce and add Parmesan cheese to taste.

Garlic bread. Spread garlic and butter on bread. Warm in oven.

NOTE: I like to serve a tossed salad either camp made or pre-packaged on the side with this meal

Venison Shepherd Pie

Ingredients:
- Two pounds of venison burger
- One large onion
- Two cans of green beans
- Two cans of tomato soup
- Two quarts of mashed potatoes

Brown venison burger in frying pan with two tablespoons of olive oil.

Brown onion separately.

Place browned venison and onion in large baking pan.

Add tomato soup, green beans and mix together with browned venison and onion.

Place on top of mixture a generous layer of mashed potatoes.

Place in oven and heat at 350 degrees for approximately 20 minutes.

Serve when potatoes are golden brown on top. Don't overcook!

Crock Pot Venison Steak

Ingredients:
- Two pounds of sliced venison steak
- One large can of tomato juice
- One small can of whole tomatoes
- One-half teaspoon of salt and one-half teaspoon of pepper
- One large onion sliced in small bits

Place steak, tomato juice, whole tomatoes, onion and salt and pepper into large crock-pot.

Cover and turn heat on low. Simmer for two to four hours or until meat is thoroughly cooked.

Serve with potatoes or rice. Season to taste.

Wild Turkey & Dumplings

Ingredients:
- Four pounds of wild turkey breast
- Two quarts boiling water
- One teaspoon salt
- One-half teaspoon pepper
- One cup of small diced potatoes
- One cup of celery cut into small bite-sized pieces
- Two chicken bullion cubes or one-half
  teaspoon of poultry seasoning
- One cup of diced carrots
- One cup of diced onions
- Dumplings

Cut turkey into bite-sized pieces. Cover with boiling water and simmer for an hour. Add the salt, pepper, and other seasoning. Cook for another hour. If (when) the water begins to boil too low, add additional water as needed. At the end of the 2 hours of boiling, add the potatoes, carrots, onions and celery. Continue cooking for another 20 minutes. During this time, prepare your dumplings.

Dumplings

Ingredients:
- One cup sifted flour
- One teaspoon baking powder
- One-half teaspoon salt
- One egg, well beaten
- One-half cup milk
- One tablespoon butter (melted)
- Parsley flakes

Sift together the flour, baking powder and the salt. Add milk to the egg; stir into the flour. Add the melted butter. Dough should be soft, but not sticky. Roll into 1" thickness. Cut with a very small ring cutter or small glass. The removable center of a doughnut cutter does very well.

When the vegetables and turkey are tender, drop the dumplings into the fast-boiling pot, cover tightly with lid and continue to simmer covered pot for ten minutes.

Serve at once with a sprinkle of parsley flakes over the top.

Venison Meatloaf

Ingredients:
- Five pounds of venison burger
- Two large onions diced
- Can of diced tomatoes
- Six slices of white bread broken into small pieces
- Three eggs
- One teaspoon of salt
- One teaspoon of pepper
- One large can of Cream of Mushroom Soup
- One package of shredded American cheese

Mix eggs, salt, pepper with a large can of Cream of Mushroom Soup. Add can of diced tomatoes and onions. Stir mixture.

Add five pounds of venison burger to mixture and stir together. Add bread to mixture. Kneed venison and bread with hands until thoroughly mixed.

Place into pre-greased bread pans (three pans). Pat down until firm.

Bake approximately one hour and 15 minutes at 375 degrees. Sprinkle cheese on top and leave in oven for 5 minutes. Cool slightly and serve with potatoes or rice.

Canned Venison*

Ingredients:
- Venison cuts from sirloin, shoulder, flank steak
- One teaspoon salt per quart of chopped venison OR
- One-half teaspoon salt per pint of chopped venison
- Quart or pint canning jars with rings and lids

Prepare venison by removing all fat and gristle. Cut meat into chunks that will fit into jars.

Pack the meat TIGHTLY in the jars. Spread the appropriate amount of salt over the top of the meat and seal the jar. (depending on quart or pint jars)

Place the filled jars in a pressure canner, with water in the bottom. Follow the guidelines for your pressure canner for the correct amount of water.

Cook for one-and-a-half hours at 15 pounds of pressure.

Turn off the heat and let the canner and the jars cool by themselves on the stove. Check the jars the next day to be certain the lids have sealed properly.

*Although not normally a process that takes place at deer camp, canned venison is one of a deer hunter's most versatile meal options. Venison is easily canned at home and transported to camp for the season. Using both pint and quart measures allows the chef to prepare meals according to the number of hunters present.

Canned venison can be made into barbecue meat spread by simply adding any of a number of commercial barbecue sauces to the meat and warming it on the stove or in the microwave. Heated alone, the canned meat makes a quick, easy and tasty sandwich, especially with tomatoes, lettuce, and onions. Warmed and served with potatoes and other vegetables, it makes a complete and delicious meal that is quickly prepared at camp.

Venison Jerky

Ingredients:
- Nine pounds of venison steak cut into 1/2 inch strips
- One-third cup of Kosher salt
- One tablespoon Garlic powder
- Two tablespoons Jerky cure
- One large tablespoon honey
- Black pepper to individual taste
- Hickory, cherry or apple wood saw dust or chips

Boil a kettle of water and dissolve garlic powder and honey in hot water. Add Jerky cure and kosher salt. Use enough water to cover meat.

Refrigerate 24 hours

Remove meat from water and sprinkle with pepper, mixing with hands. Sprinkle a second time and mix by hand, adding pepper to suit individual tastes

Hang meat strips vertically from wire racks in a small smoker. Avoid over handling meat

Place wood chips or saw dust over burner and add heat until wood begins smoking.

Let meat smoke until wood or dust has gone. Use enough wood to create plenty of smoke.

Raise temperature to 200-250 degrees and maintain that level. Check after 2 hours and every half-hour thereafter until done.

Total smoking and cooking time is approximately 4-5 hours.

Makes about 4 pounds of Jerky

Camp members make sauerkraut for a November dinner.

Roasted Wild Turkey

Ingredients:
- One large skinned wild turkey
- One tablespoon salt
- One tablespoon pepper
- One large diced onion
- One cup of diced celery
- Four slices of white bread
- One package of stove top turkey stuffing
- One cooking bag for turkey

Mix stove top turkey dressing together according to directions on box. Heat and cool.

Add one cup of diced onion and one cup of diced celery to mixture. Add four slices of white bread broken into small bits.

Stuff turkey cavity with dressing mixture.

Place stuffed turkey into cooking bag and sprinkle with salt and pepper. Close bag and place in large electric turkey roaster.

Add water to roaster and close cover. Cook turkey for four hours or until tender. Check to see that water does not evaporate from roaster.

Serve roasted turkey with potatoes, vegetables, salad and cranberry sauce.

Rice and Venison with Gravy

Ingredients:
- Two pounds of venison steak
- Two packages of brown gravy mix
- Two cups of white rice
- One quarter cup of olive oil
- Six and one-half cups of water

Cut the venison steaks into small, bit-size cubes

Boil water and stir in white rice. Cook approximately 15 minutes on low heat.

Place olive oil in frying pan and stir in venison cubes. Stir slowly until brown.

Add two packages of brown gravy mix and one-half cup of water.

Bring venison/gravy mixture to slow boil until gravy thickens

Scope rice onto plates and add mixture of venison steak and gravy mixture

CHAPTER 11

Equipment –
Clothes, Footwear, and Rifle

*C*amp arguments and often-heated debates occur when hunters voice their opinions on the best clothing, footwear, and rifle that should be used while hunting deer. These friendly discussions can occasionally turn fiery and emotional as each sportsman defends his or her personal choice of hunting gear.

Clearly, each hunter's personal experiences are reflected in these discussions. The subject of the best equipment to use is often sacred ground for deer hunters. All have their favorites.

Additionally, many nimrods are ritualistic about their equipment and clothing. Personally, I have worn the same Woolrich hunting pants for over 20 years. I am admittedly superstitious about these pants, as I believe they bring me good luck. I keep the pants in a plastic bag of pine boughs for two weeks prior to the season opener to help eliminate most of the human scent on the wool.

After many years as an ardent deer hunter, personal guide and student of the whitetail deer, I have reached the conclusion that there is definitely a list of best equipment to be used by the successful hunter. This list might be challenged (I can almost guarantee it!) by other ardent hunters willing to defend their positions.

These choices will obviously vary from hunter to hunter, climate to climate, and region to region, but one thing is perfectly clear: members at our camp who annually shoot a trophy deer display common elements in their selection of clothes, footwear and rifle.

Brand, style and selection can fall into several categories. For example some hunters prefer wool clothing. Others like flannel and still others choose cotton. Regardless, all our hunters buy quality clothing that provides the common elements of warmth, comfort and soundless movement.

This chapter will discuss some basic fundamentals of rifle and equipment selection. Arguably tainted by my many years in the woods, I will offer my best opinions and suggestions for your consideration.

These suggestions can be used as a framework to help you select the most appropriate clothing, footwear, rifle and related equipment you need to challenge the whitetail deer. I hope these guidelines will assist you in getting that trophy buck.

First, as noted, begin by choosing clothes that are warm, quiet and comfortable. Clothes that scratch, squeak or crinkle will alert deer to danger. These noisy types of clothing do more to scare Michigan deer than anything I can think of outside of singing in the deer stand. (See Rule #5 in Chapter 8.)

My personal preference for outerwear is either wool or polar fleece. These soft materials are quiet and retain body heat. Long hours spent in your hunting stand can result in chills. This you do not need. Many companies market quality wool or polar fleece products. My favorites include Woolrich, L.L. Bean and Cabela's, to name a few.

Many quality wool products can also be purchased in chain stores or malls. Most companies provide catalogs of varying styles, sizes and selection needed by the astute woodsman.

Wosterlon is another excellent, soft material for hunting clothing. Polar fleece with Gore-Tex is another good choice.

I always layer my clothing when preparing for the hunt. This allows me to shed clothing if the weather warms. The layering also provides space to trap air and retain body heat in colder conditions.

You can take clothes off in the woods if the weather gets warm, but you can't add clothes if you get cold. Dressing warmly through layering is an appropriate given for the successful deer hunter.

If the weather forecast includes the chance of rain, I always add a Gore-Tex jacket and hat to my daypack. The following is a listing of my personal choices of hunting clothes.

Clothing Selection

My first item of clothing is a good set of Duafold or Cabela's MTP polyester-spandex underwear. The wicking effect of these modern day materials makes a marvelous difference from the days when we used cotton long johns that quickly grew damp with sweat when walking to our blinds. They remained wet and clammy all day. Ugh!

Rick Mills and his buck shot in 1999.

I prefer the two-piece to the one-piece style of long underwear. However, this selection is a matter of personal choice. Be sure your underwear is loose fitting so you can move freely in your hunting stand.

Over this loose fitting, long underwear I wear a long-sleeve cotton turtleneck. This allows me to keep my neck area warm and provides a soft, quiet barrier for my hunting shirts.

On top of this cotton turtleneck I wear a Pendelton wool shirt. I prefer wool because it is very quiet and maintains warmth and body heat even if wet. Following my wool shirt, I put on a loose fitting flannel shirt — usually red, but the color is not critically important. Several manufacturers make orange flannel shirts. My choice of flannel shirt manufacturers is either Woolrich or L.L. Bean.

On top of my flannel shirt, I prefer a heavy, green-and-black-colored Woolrich shirt. The green and black color provides great camouflage while I sit in my stand. Over this wool shirt I wear an orange insulated vest. I prefer goose-down or polar fleece materials.

My favorite vest is Thinsulate-insulated and reversible orange and camouflage in color.

This combination allows me to use the same vest for both bow and rifle hunting.

My hunting pants are red-and-black Woolrich wool, with suspenders and a large belt. I have worn the same pants for over 20 years. These well-made pants are excellent for cold weather. If the weather is mild, I choose either a light green wool pant from Filson or a lighter wool pant made in Johnson, Vermont. Both are green in color. In mild weather, I wear a pair of six-pocket cotton camouflage pants.

The above combination allows me to adjust my layering according to the weather conditions. On very cold days I exchange the vest for a goose-down parka in camouflage color. I always wear an orange vest outer garment for safety.

My headgear is either a lined camouflage style baseball hat, with earflaps, or a fur-lined mountie style hat for colder weather. My head-wear depends on the weather. In rainy weather, I choose a Gore-Tex lined, waterproof hat. When bow hunting, I prefer a camouflage hat with mesh head-net attached. Many manufactures make the above items.

Footwear

Take care of your feet and they'll take care of you! When going hunting, I pay special attention to my footwear.

First I put on a pair of soft cotton wicking type sweat socks. Some hunters prefer polypropylene socks, but I like cotton exercise type socks. Over these cotton socks I wear a good quality wool sock that is loosely fitted. The cotton sweat sock is excellent for cushioning your feet. The heavy pair of wool socks keeps your toes warm. Both Cabela's and L.L. Bean offer an excellent wool sock. This new Smart Wool is wonderful!

I hate cold feet and will keep my feet warm. Don't skimp on quality footwear of any kind. From socks to boots, use the best.

My selection of boots falls into one of three types, depending on the weather.

MILD WEATHER. I wear rubber bottom, leather top, ten inch L.L. Bean boots. These are the Maine Guide type boots that have been marketed for many years. The rubber bottom is nearly scent free and provides ease of walking to and from my hunting stands.

COOLER WEATHER. My choice for near freezing temperatures is Rocky Bear Claw boots with 800 grams of thinsulite insulation. My personal preference is brown camouflage.

FREEZING WEATHER. The LaCrosse rubber packs in either the sorrel type with felt liners or an all-rubber LaCrosse felt pac rated to minus 8l below zero are my favorites under extreme conditions.

Keeping your feet warm and dry is obviously the key to avoiding cold toes. Warm feet allow you to sit in comfort for long hours in the woods. Cold toes make your hunt miserable.

As a 14-year-old hunter I wore a pair of leather, lace-to-the-top hunting boots. I never had colder feet. Following that experience I chose felts covered with rubber boots. This was the choice of footwear for many veteran hunters at the time. I learned quickly, as a young hunter, about proper clothing and footwear.

When hunting in a wet, swampy area I wear LaCrosse insulated rubber knee high boots or insulated, ankle fitting, hip boots depending on the depth of the water. These type boots have proved invaluable in keeping my feet warm and dry in wet swampy areas located on our Pine Hill Club property.

Whatever footgear you choose, be certain it is comfortable to walk in, warm and waterproof. Cold, wet feet can ruin your day in the woods and result in bad memories of your day in the field. Take care of your toes!

As I have shared in earlier chapters, I also always carry a daypack when I am deer hunting. My preference is a waterproof camouflage color daypack that has at least two large storage areas for assorted equipment. I use polar fleece as it is quiet and does not scratch on the brush when I am walking to and from my hunting blind.

Items I include in my daypack are listed below: All have a purpose and provide me with the necessary equipment for a comfortable and successful day in the woods.

Daypack essentials

- A twelve-foot length of strong rope.
- A small sharp knife, with a three to three and one-half inch-locking blade. (I prefer the Buck Folding Hunter 110 model)
- A small Mini-Mag flashlight with extra batteries.
- One extra pair each of cotton and wool socks
- One extra pair of gloves (Mittens are my choice in extremely cold weather)
- Extra shells carried in a leather pouch or cartridge holder (Ten shells maximum)
- Three candy bars, two packs of chewing gum and a handful of hard candy.
- Thermos of hot black coffee
- Two sandwiches wrapped in plastic
- Compass, matches, toilet paper. (I place my toilet paper in a waterproof, zip-lock bag)
- One small bottle of water and one soda
- Buck lure and scent block spray
- One small pair of eight power binoculars
- A small roll of duct tape
- Plastic bag and rubber gloves
- Reading materials (usually left in my blind before opening day)

Properly clothed and carrying a filled daypack and loaded rifle, I am ready to take to the woods in pursuit of the mighty whitetail.

Careful selection of quality equipment makes your hunt more comfortable, enjoyable and successful. Don't skimp on good equipment as cheap is not always better.

Selecting your Deer Rifle

Selecting a whitetail deer rifle is much like the choosing the best automobile. Many factors go into the selection of the proper rifle, not the least of which is personal preference.

We hunt in a rifle zone at the Pine Hill Club. While shotguns are also legal weapons in our hunting area, all our members use a rifle.

My comments in this book will be directed to rifle hunters. If you hunt in a shotgun only zone, consider a weapon that includes a rifled barrel for more accurate shooting, is fast handling and utilizes a low power scope. I do not offer a breakdown of shotguns in this book, but the suggestions for shooting apply equally to either a rifle or shotgun.

Serious hunters should ask themselves several questions when considering what deer rifle they want to use.

"What type of terrain do you plan to hunt?"

"Do you favorite open sights or telescopic sights?"

"How recoil sensitive are you when shooting a rifle?"

"What rifle weight is comfortable for you to carry?"

"What action do you prefer?" (bolt, lever, auto-loader or pump)

"Are you right handed or left-handed?"

The questions for the discriminating hunter could go on and on when selecting the proper rifle or shotgun.

Typical comments heard in our deer camp include:

"I can shoot this rifle better than any other I have tried."

"My father swears by this rifle."

"Bolt actions rifles are more accurate than any other option."

Such comments among hunters can go on for hours as they debate the "best" deer rifle.

In this section I will give you my advice and opinion, garnered after almost fifty years of whitetail hunting. This advice is based on extensive reading, field-testing of hundreds of rifles and most importantly what seems to put venison on the buck pole.

Obviously, choosing the right rifle for you makes your hunt more enjoyable and increases your odds for success. Consider fit, sights, weight, action and caliber. You must also choose a weapon that is matched to your needs and the terrain you hunt.

Don't choose a flat-shooting, high velocity rifle for brush hunting. Such a weapon may be excellent for open cover and long-range shooting conditions, but it will not perform well in thick, heavy, dense brush.

Always match your rifle and bullet selection to the environment and the game you seek.

My personal preferences for the Pine Hill Club property fall into several calibers and actions, given our varying terrain and hunting options.

I recommend four basic caliber's: .270 Winchester with 130 grain bullets, 30-06 Springfield with 180 grain bullets, .308 Winchester with 150 grain bullets and the 7mm Remington magnum with 175 grain bullets. My .30-.30 carbine is loaded with 170-grain bullets. The above selections are my personal favorites for whitetail hunting.

My action of preference is the tried and true bolt action.

While I have killed many deer with the .30-.30 Winchester, lever-action, timber rifle, I am convinced it is not the best choice for the discriminating shooter. This rifle has provided me with many long tracks seeking to recover wounded deer, however, a flatter shooting, higher velocity rifle would have probably secured these deer more quickly and without lengthy tracks.

For me, the most important factor to consider, no matter which caliber or model rifle you chose, is can you shoot the rifle accurately?

Many beginners I have guided can't hit the inside of a barn. In this case, no caliber or action will work well. Veteran and inexperienced hunters alike will miss many chances at bagging their buck, even when they practice shooting and are good marksmen. These folks who don't practice and can't shoot accurately shouldn't hunt.

Deer have plenty of room around them. The kill zone is a relatively small 8 to 12 inches. I also have missed bucks with all of the above listed calibers. In every case, it was due to excitement, rushing my shot or good, old-fashioned buck fever.

The most skilled hunters will miss at times. The miss is almost never the fault of the rifle.

While some exceptions do occur though misfires, broken scope wires, faulty fire-pins or a damaged sight, such a miss is almost always due to shooter error.

The successful deer hunter should always remember some simple but critical rules when selecting the best rifle for his use in whitetail hunting.

Rules to Remember About Rifles

Rule # 1. Don't buy a rifle just to look at. Successful hunters use their rifles and are familiar with the shouldering, safety and sight picture. Whether the stock is glossy, dull, synthetic or wood doesn't really matter. Whether the action is a pump, lever or bolt action is not critically important.

What matters is does the rifle fit you personally and do you have confidence in the weapon?

The basic question always becomes, "Can you shoot the rifle quickly and accurately?" If not, you have the wrong weapon for you!

Rule # 2. Have you checked the trigger pull on your rifle? Hunting rifles should have a three or four pound, crisp trigger pull. Any gunsmith with a trigger gauge can adjust your trigger pull to these specifications. Rifles with a stiff or creepy trigger pull throw the shooter off and accuracy suffers. This usually results in a missed or poorly placed shot. Always begin your quest for accuracy with a crisp trigger pull.

Rule # 3. My next bit of advice is for the hunter to control the recoil on your rifle. Can you accurately shoot your rifle without flinching? No matter how good your rifle, if you flinch or jump prior to squeezing the trigger, you will not shoot accurately or obtain close, tight shot groupings.

Many vendors can modify recoil. My favorite process is to have a rifle Mag-na-ported. Mag-na-port Corporation in Mt. Clemens, Michigan, is expert in recoil reduction. (The address for Mag-na-port Corporation is listed in the appendix.)

Another option for the discriminating hunter is the addition of a muzzle brake to reduce recoil and barrel jump. Adding a muzzle brake to your rifle will usually add two inches to the barrel length. However, this process does a great job of reducing recoil.

A third option is to add a thick, rubber recoil pad. This usually requires the stock to be shortened because of the thickness of the added pad. (I personally don't like to cut off a stock.)

Rule # 4. Buy quality scope mounts for your rifle. An expensive scope mounted on cheap, low quality scope mounts will negatively affect accuracy.

I believe you are better served with a low-priced scope on good mounts than the reverse. Get good scope mounts for your rifle and you will not be sorry. Many manufactures such as Leopold, Redfield or Millet market quality scope mounts for the discriminating hunter.

Rule # 5. Select good quality optics to go with your quality scope mounts. The old adage that you get what you pay for applies to selecting a scope. Personally, I don't buy the most expensive scopes because I don't feel they add that much to your accuracy. My wallet is not ready for a cash outlay of $1,000 to $1,200 for a scope.

I do believe expensive scopes are wonderful, if you can afford them. However, for my money I prefer the Leopold Var X-III as the best value for the money. A close, if not equal, second choice is the Nikon Monarch scope in variable power.

Both scope selections have performed flawlessly for me over many years of hunting the elusive whitetail.

Most hunters know that the larger the objective, the more light is gathered in the scope. This factor allows added time for hunting in the early morning light and at dusk.

However, because the larger the size of the objective, for example, 50-mm, the higher the scope must be mounted on the rifle, requiring the shooter to lift his head on the stock of the rifle. Such action, even though slight, decreases accuracy in my opinion.

My personal preference is a 40-44 mm objective. These scopes mount tight to the rifle and afford the shooter a straight-sight picture. Keeping my head down on the stock of the rifle is my preferred method of shooting accurately.

As noted earlier in this book, I don't like see-thru mounts. Though arguable, this is my preference. If you prefer a see-thru mount and can shoot accurately with them, more power to you. Accurate shooting is the key to bagging your buck.

What Caliber is Best?

Caliber selection is a debatable issue among almost all serious deer hunters. Any of the calibers listed earlier will perform well on the white-tail deer. Other selections might be added. For instance, I would include these additional calibers for your consideration. The 7mm Mauser, .280,

25-06, 7mm-08, .243 and the big bore 45-70 all have been most successful in bagging deer.

Some of my friends believe the .300 Winchester magnum and the
.338 Winchester magnum are also quality deer guns. It is my personal
opinion these calibers are normally too big for hunting whitetail deer
and are prone to having massive, hurtful recoil. Again, if you can shoot
accurately, these magnum calibers are certainly effective on whitetails.

In an attempt not to offend anyone and to draw closure to the selection of the "best" deer rifle, I will offer my personal list of favorites. I
presently own at least one of all the rifles listed below and have shot
many deer with each.

With sincere apologies to all hunters who don't agree, my list includes:

Bob's Favorite Deer Rifles

- Remington 700 in the Classic. Caliber .270 with Nikon Monarch
  5.5-16.5 power scope in 44 mm objective.
- Remington 700 in the Classic. Caliber 30-06 with Leopold Var X-III
  in 3-9 power scope in 50 mm objective.
- Ruger M-77 in wood finish. Caliber 30-06 with Redfield, WA 2-7
  power scope in 40 mm objective.
- Winchester M-70 in Featherweight Classic wood. Caliber 30-06
  with Redfield, WA 2-7 power scope in 40 mm objective.
- Ruger M-77 in wood finish. Caliber .308 with Redfield, WA 2-7
  power scope in 40 mm objective.
- Winchester M-94 carbine. Caliber .30-.30 with open sights.

My list could go on and on, but the listed six rifles above have been
good to me throughout my years as a whitetail hunter and guide. I will
yield that other selections could be added, as the debate about the best
deer rifle is unending.

Personally, I don't believe there is any one best deer rifle. Rifle selection is a personal choice for each and every hunter. The rifle and caliber
you shoot most accurately is the best one for you, regardless of what
anyone else recommends.

For many years, as a young hunter, I carried the Winchester .30-.30
carbine in lever action. It was the "gun that won the west". At the time,

every true deer hunter wanted a Winchester .30-.30. I was no exception. When I was 14 years old, this rifle sold used for $25-35 dollars. A new model was $64.00. I still hunt with my first .30-.30 Winchester. It is as accurate and good today as it was the day I bought it in 1954.

Another rifle that I used extensively was a Remington Model 7400 in semi-auto loader in the .308 caliber. I shot many deer with this rifle. However, for me it did not perform well. In my opinion, the trigger pull was sloppy and the rifle tended to jam in cold weather conditions.

In my midyears of hunting, I switched to a Savage Model 99 lever action, chambered for the .300 Savage cartridge. This is a hard hitting, reasonably fast-operating rifle. It is most adequate for hunting the whitetail.

Bob Mills with favorite Winchester 30-30's.

For the past twenty-five years, I have been a bolt action shooter. I like the crisp trigger pull, dependability of the action and the accuracy this type of rifle can produce both on the target range and in the field. My favorite deer rifle is the bolt action in the .270 caliber. The bolt action 30-06 is an equally solid choice.

Regardless of your choice, your first shot is the one that most always puts venison on the buck pole! Do it right!

I will cheerfully agree with any hunter who disapproves of my list. I will, however, defend my recommendations by citing many successful hunts and experience in guiding hunters of all ages.

My close personal friend and hunting partner, Roger Dixon, once shot an antelope in Wyoming at a distance of over 400 yards with a bolt-action Winchester Model 70 rifle in the 30-06 caliber. This shot reaffirmed my belief in the accuracy and dependability of the bolt action.

Simply put, shoot what you are confident with and can comfortably shoot accurately. Buy a rifle that you like to shoot and practice often. Confidence in your rifle is critical for bagging that trophy buck.

Good Hunting!

Velocity Statistics

Caliber/Bullet	100 yards	200 yards	300 yards
.270 (130 grain)	2776	2510	2259
30-06 (180 grain)	2348	2023	1727
.308 (180 grain)	2393	2178	1974
.30-.30 (170 grain)	1895	1619	1381
7mm Mag (175 grain)	2645	2440	2244

Buck shot by Tom Tillman. Note width of rack.

CHAPTER 12

Deer Camp – 'More than Killing Deer'

*I*n *Deer Camp – An American Tradition,* I have attempted to capture the unique nature and spirit of a private hunting camp, the Pine Hill Club. My goal has been to create for you an accurate picture that depicts our love of the out-of-doors and our special yearning for a simpler way of life.

Our ancestors took to the woods to become one with nature, to learn the meaning of the deer's daily movements and to follow their trails as they completed their life cycle. It is that quest that members of a hunting camp experience and only a deer hunter can truly understand.

At the Pine Hill Club, we leave our complicated, computer-based, technological world for one of simpler pleasures. For a few days each year, we are relieved of our worries, whatever they may be. The sound of the wind in the trees and the smell of wood burning in the campfire uplift our souls. Though tired, we return to the cabin each evening invigorated and renewed by nature's wonders.

Deer camps are filled with strong traditions and years of special events collectively form deep, lasting bonds between members. Various types of hunting camps have existed since people banded together to hunt for food.

These special gatherings create a common unity and collective memory among members.

Individuals seek to create or join private hunting camps for a variety of reasons: safety, camaraderie and the joy of sharing the great outdoors.

Some members join or buy a deer camp only to play cards, sit by the fire or get away from the stress of jobs. These individuals find relaxation and joy in being out-of-doors. Others pursue the art of hunting, becoming a student of the sport, while seeking the very special and primal thrill of the chase.

Whether the deer camp is a trailer located on a few private acres, a tent on state land or a log cabin makes little difference. All camps exist for outdoorsmen to share quality time in the woods.

Residuals of a Deer Camp

Strong bonds and mutual friendships are formed through membership in a private camp, which offers many added benefits besides providing a place to shoot deer..

At the Pine Hill Club, camp members and their wives have opportunities to pick berries, hunt for mushrooms, go cross country skiing, and hiking on the trails provided. These activities are an added incentive to being a member of a private camp.

Many camp members will schedule hunting trips and fishing ventures together in other states during the off season for deer. Our camp members have hunted together for antelope in Wyoming, as well as caribou in Alaska. We have fished together throughout the North American continent from Lake Michigan to Alaska's Kenai River.

These common outdoor adventures have only served to cement the bonds among our "circle of steel". As a private camp, we are like family, sharing common purpose and common bonds.

Some of our members vacation in the winter together and share dinners and other family events with one another during the off-season. The list of communal activities could go on and on.

Most club members share pictures of previous hunts or e-mail information to one another during the off-season. Like close families, they form a support base to help each other whether in time of need or to collectively celebrate a wedding, the birth of a new child or a recent retirement.

Information and resources are shared among members about everything from re-loading equipment to plumbing. All members in our camp freely share with one another their varied, professional expertise.

Tom Olson plays a song for members around the camp fire after opening day.

The wives of members also get to know each other and our extended family grows with each member added.

Young hunters – a New Generation

The Pine Hill Club is a camp for families. Most members bring their children to camp to share in work day or off-season activities. A summer pig roast allows our families to gather for food, fun and old-fashioned games. Horseshoes, sack races and hayrides are but a few examples.

Our membership includes many father-son combinations. The Tyler family has a grandfather, father and son hunting at the camp. Members display a sincere joy of the woods and freely share stories about past events. Our members are dedicated sportsmen, supporting Quality Deer Management practices and proven conservation programs.

Suggestions and advice are exchanged between members with special focus on the young children who will be our future hunters.

My oldest grandson, Jake, will be able to bow hunt this year. All camp members are excited about sharing with him the skills needed for a successful hunt. Together, we are planning on building Jake his personal bow stand this coming summer.

Our camp manager, Bruce Anderson, has a young son named Cody, who is proficient in shooting targets with both a .22 rifle and small bore shotgun. The supervised camp environment provides Cody with a structured, safe setting to develop his shooting skills. Bruce has taken his son on many hunts. Together they have sat in the blind and watched for deer while both bow and rifle hunting. Bruce has shot many bucks with Cody by his side.

Additionally, our son Dave takes his three sons hunting. Grandsons Jake, Joe and Matt appear eager and ready to become partners in the camp. Jamie Dixon's son Bradley loves fresh venison and revels in the out-of-doors. Only time and practice will develop their skills as hunters, trackers and students of the whitetail.

Safety at Deer Camp

All camp members preach and practice safety. Rules for safe gun handling are embedded in the soul of every member. No loaded gun is ever allowed in the cabin. All hunters must wear hunter orange when hunting and all guns must be unloaded and cased when in a vehicle.

Members are not allowed to take alcohol into the woods. Everyone hunting on our property, member and guest alike observe this sacred rule.

I deal with any violation of this rule in a stern and swift manner. We have lost one member due to this policy. I don't apologize. All know the rules of the camp.

In addition, all members must sign a release of liability form before they join the camp. Membership in the Pine Hill Club is by invitation only. New members are carefully screened before being asked to join our group. All are given a copy of the camp rules. These rules are annually reviewed at the dinner table on opening night. Questions are answered and suggestions welcomed.

We have a standing list of prospective members, as many other hunters seek the safety and security of a proven private club. Members pay a small yearly fee to cover the property taxes, insurance, maintenance and other overall costs of operating the camp.

Young children of members are taught how to use a BB gun safely and are taught a respect for the game they will eventually seek. We observe safety at all times. The continual stressing of safety is a permanent reminder for the welfare of all. This message is etched on the brain of every member in our camp.

I strongly believe that you can never stress safety too much. It is a constant at the Pine Hill Club.

Why Go to Deer Camp?

This past season member Bert Palmer and I reflected on the reasons we go to deer camp.

The electricity and magnetism of a deer camp are hard to describe in words. The heart-pounding excitement of the hunters anticipating opening day, the stories of past hunts relived in specific detail, shared experiences, and the good-natured arguments over the best deer rifle or the best hunting tactics highlight the long list of jovial fun shared by our membership.

The Pine Hill Club consists of 21 men, with widely varying professions and backgrounds, who hunt on 760 acres of property. The camp has existed for nearly 30 years. Over half the hunters have more than 20 years of woods experience hunting whitetail deer at the camp.

On the eve of the hunting season, a home-cooked dinner is catered by Tom and Carol Biersbach. Camp rules are reviewed with members and special events of the

Member Wayne Coston enjoying a game of euchre. Note Dave's Quiver.

past year are recognized. Every member is expected to reflect on the past year and a special bonding occurs. Job changes, awards received, retirements, and anniversaries are shared with the group. The dinner is a kick-off to the hunt and is a special event for all in the camp. Jokingly, neckties are required with hunting shirts at this more formal dinner.

Without question, hunters take to the woods in pursuit of the elusive whitetail buck.

However, killing a deer is not the crucial factor that brings our hunters to camp each fall.

For the record, the Pine Hill Club hunters do indeed harvest deer on the property. Since the camp was purchased in 1972, our hunters have shot over 400 deer. This past season twenty-three deer were harvested, with bucks being six-point or bigger.

The Pine Hill Club, which originally began as a bucks-only camp, now tries to balance our buck kill with the shooting of one doe per buck. Quality Deer management experts support this 50-50 ratio. Only mature does are harvested.

No deer drives occur and spikes, four pointers and button bucks are now allowed to grow into six, eight and ten point bucks. All members see many deer and support the six-point rule, which we instituted in the fall of 1999.

Camp life consists of large meals, lots of euchre games, and many stories. A closeness of purpose is shared among the members. Camp life is one of harmony and serenity that comes along with the savory smell of bacon frying, the warmth of a glowing wood and the excitement of a winning hand in a friendly card game.

Members Bert Palmer and Dick Tyler congratulate each other on getting their deer.

World problems are solved with the wisdom of camp veterans and the energy of youth adds a special flavor to the seasoned hunters with many kills to their credit. Debates are frequent and friendly ribbing and jokes are part of camp-life.

Joe Mills argues that the 7mm Mag. is the best caliber for deer hunting. Al Quick agrees, because he shoots a 7mm Mag. Ron Williams, Dave Mills and Roger Dixon disagree, as they use the 30-06 caliber and feel this is the perfect caliber for hunting the whitetail. Bob Mills and Bert Palmer swear by the .270 caliber. The argument never reaches closure and annually occurs when our hunters get together in pursuit of the mighty buck.

Snoring in the bunkhouse is always a topic at the morning coffee table with Kirk Coston and Jim Ward leading the pack of jokes about "chain-saw" members. Issues from politics, economics and football games surround the breakfast table discussion.

The camp consists of a large cabin that sleeps sixteen hunters with complete cooking facilities, refrigerator and all the amenities needed to accommodate the group.

The smell of gun oil, boot grease and coffee brewing is ever present. A separate bunkhouse sleeps seven other members and features running water and a bathroom. Heat is provided by four wall-heaters plus a stone fireplace built from rocks taken from the property.

Members sharpening knives always generate interest about the best knife for deer hunting. Dave Mills swears by a Browning knife, Bruce Anderson likes the folding Buck knife, and several members choose the Marble Fieldcraft as the ultimate tool for cleaning a deer.

Members kid each other about balding, gaining weight, vehicles purchased, or deer missed from previous years. The best boots, scopes and other equipment are always topics of discussion.

Horns from previous seasons and pictures adorn the cabin wall with momentos collected over the many years of the camp existence.

Our camp is a typical Michigan deer camp. Harvesting a deer is truly only one small part of why hunters take to the woods in the fall each year.

Good times in a hunting camp are measured by more than the number of deer killed. The laughter, camaraderie and excitement surrounding the opening day of a new season annually provide heart-warming lists of quality memories. Tagging the buck is only the "frosting on the cake" for our members.

Opening evening is very special. Successful hunters return at dark with their bucks. Stories, laughter and friendly debates start all over again. The crackling fire and a hot meal cap off a relaxing day in the woods.

The collegiality of old friends and camp-life make each season more than I can describe in words. Only when a hunter experiences such an old-fashioned deer camp atmosphere can he truly appreciate the challenge of the whitetail buck.

The joy we share in camp life, regardless of age or profession, is the magnet that brings our members back to the camp.

Concluding Thoughts

Yes, a hunting camp is much more than killing deer! My heartfelt prayer is that the sundry traditions and multiple joys of shared outdoors experiences will continue for you and for all future generations.

I wish you success on all your upcoming hunting trips. May the buck of your dreams soon become a reality!

While I hope some of the tips and ideas shared herein will help you become a more successful deer hunter, I hope even more that the basic concept of a shared love of the out-of-doors came through in this book.

Good Hunting!

Cabin with first addition (Note stove pipe through roof). Three more additions followed.

ABOUT THE AUTHOR

Author beside buck pole. Another successful hunting season at the Pine Hill Club.

Robert (Bob) Mills developed a passion for hunting and the great out-of-doors at a very early age. The Mills Family lived in the country where hunting was a family affair and way of life.

Bob's father Clayton, Grandfather Harry and numerous uncles – Vern, Fieldyn, Wayne, Ron, and Mac – all loved to hunt the magnificent whitetail deer. His mother Edna, sister Mary Ester and numerous aunts and cousins all enjoyed the sport of deer hunting and fishing as well.

The Mills' family reunions always revolved around three things: (1) lots of food and refreshments; (2) laughter and singing, with Grandmother Anna playing the piano; and (3) stories of hunting and fishing adventures.

Uncle Vern, in particular, would share deer hunting stories in a most descriptive, humorous and comical manner. With his engaging grin, huge smile and big bushy eyebrows dancing, he related the exact details of his hunting adventures in a manner designed to delight young and old alike.

Bob grew up with a rifle in his hand, borrowing his grandfather's .22 rifle in pursuit of squirrels and rabbits that were found in abundance in the woods on the family farm near Millington, Michigan.

He participated in his first deer hunt in 1950 with his father Clayton. From that time on, he counted the days until he could buy a hunting license. There was no doubt he would be in the deer woods with his father, mother, sister, uncles and grandfather when he was 14 and could legally hunt deer in Michigan.

Proudly carrying a borrowed 12-gauge, double -barrel Savage/Stevens shotgun, loaded with slugs, on that opening morning, 1953, near Gladwin, Michigan, a large eight-point buck walked near his stand and presented him with a shot. However, like many first-time hunters, Bob did not succeed in taking that first buck, which still haunts his dreams. Another hunter tagged "his" trophy. No other opportunities presented themselves that initial season.

The following year, Bob purchased his first deer rifle: a .30-.30-caliber bolt Stevens/Savage for the grand sum of $27.00. Like many of us from this era, he remembers buying the gun for $1.00 down and $1.00 per week, until it was paid for in full.

On the same spot where he saw his first buck, he shot a three-pointer with his new rifle the following year. This was his first of many whitetail bucks. His father Clayton was present in camp for this very special moment. Like all parents in history, he was extremely proud of his son's first deer.

The next year Bob bought his second deer rifle – a much-cherished .32 Special Winchester Model 94 lever action. The gun cost $50 and Bob bagged 13 deer over the coming years with this timber rifle.

As he grew older, so did his passion for deer hunting. For eight years Bob served as a caretaker/guide at the Willing Ranch, a private, deer camp of 3,000 acres, which hosted a total of 50 hunters. He checked deer, tracked wounded deer and always managed to shoot a buck with his trusty Winchester.

In 1972 he purchased 80 acres of private land in Isabella County with his long-time friend and hunting partner Alan Quick. The 80 acres became known as the Pine Hill Club, because of the large White Pine trees on the top of the hill next to the camp's entrance. This property became the focal point for many years of great hunting and stories about deer hunting.

Robert Mills is a professor of school administration by training, but his passion for deer hunting has been the lodestone of his life. He has taught hunter safety classes, become skilled with the bow and muzzle-loader, and has developed into a tireless tracker of wounded deer.

"He literally smells deer," observe friends, who have shared long, challenging tracks with him.

Having served as a hunting guide throughout his life, helping young hunters take their first deer has become his greatest thrill. In this regard, his four sons have provided him with many unique and memorable opportunities as a mentor and coach.

Over the years, more than 400 deer have been harvested at the Pine Hill Club. Bob can recall most of the hunts and savors the true stories found in this book.

With nearly 50 years of woods experience under his belt, he knows deer hunting and the secrets of success. Additionally, he has authored many articles about hunting and the great out-of-doors.

His trophies include numerous whitetail bucks, black bear, antelope and caribou. He still awaits the elusive Alaskan Moose.

Robert C. Mills knows deer hunting and his first book *DEER CAMP – An American Tradition* summarizes his many years of guiding both beginners and veterans, managing the natural resources and operating a successful old-fashioned deer camp in northern Michigan.

In this book, Bob attempts to address the question of why so many people of such varying backgrounds — professionally, culturally, socially and academically — leave their comfortable homes and make an annual pilgrimage to deer camp, where they bond in a manner unique to societal norms.

Bob's favorite quote, to young and old, is, "Let the buck pole do the talking".

SELECTED REFERENCES

Using the Internet opens up a world of references for the discriminating hunter.

Below is a listing of selected web sites for possible further references.

Web Sites

Accurate Arms co. Inc www.accuratepowder.com
Ammo Depot www.ammodepot.com
Big Bore bullets of Alaska www.awloo.com/bbb/index.htm
Brenneke of America Ltd. Turpin@theriver.com
Cheaper than Dirt www.cheaperthandirt.com
Leupold www.leupold.com
Denver bullet Co. denbullets@aol.com
Dynamit Nobel RWS Inc. www.dnrws.com
Elephant Black Powder www.elephantblackpowder.com
Federal Cartridge Co. www.federalcartridge.com
Hornady www.hornady.com
Ace Case Co. www.acecase.com
Lyman www.lymanproducts.com
Nosler bullets Inc. www.nosler.com
Remington www.remington.com
Boyt Harness Co. www.boytharness.com
Nikon Inc. www.nikonusa.com
Williams gun Sight Co. www.williamsgunsight.com
Winchester Safes www.fireking.com
Mag-Na-Port Int'l Inc. www.magnaport.com
Outers www.outers-guncare.com
Silencio www.silencio.com
Knight Rifles www.knightrifles.com
Marlin www.marlinfirearms.com
Federeal Arms www.fedarms.com
Hastings barrels www.hastingsbarrels.com
Winchester Firearms www.winchester-guns.com
Bianchi www.bianchiint.com
Hunter Co. www.huntercompany.com
Gun List www.gunlist.com
GUNS Magazine www.gunsmagazine.com
Lee Precision, Inc. www.leeprecision.com
Thompson Center Arms www.tcarms.com
Sports Afield www.sportsafield.comm
The Gun Journal www.shooters.com
Marble Arms www.marblearms.com

Books

Blackpowder Loading Manual, 3rd Edition, by Sam Fadala, DBI Books, a division of Krause Publications, Iola, WI 1995. 368 pp., illus.

Bolt Action Rifles, 3rd Edition, by Frank de Haas, DBI Books, a division of Krause Publications, Iola, WI, 1995. 528 pp., illus.

Bowhunter's Handbook, Expert Strategies and Techniques, by M.R. James with Fred Asbell, Dave Holt, Dwight Schuh & Dave Samuel, DBI Books, a division of Krause Publications, Iola, WI, 1997. 256pp.,illus.

The Complete Venison Cookbook from Field to Table, by Jim & Ann Casada, Krause Publications, Iola, WI, 1996. 208 pp.

Deer and Deer Hunting: The Serious Hunter's Guide, by Dr. Robert Wegner, Stackpole Books, Harrisburg, PA, 1984. 384 pp., illus.

Encyclocpedia of Deer, by G. Kenneth Whitehead, Safari Press, Huntington, CA, 1993. 704 pp., illus.

Great Michigan Deer Tales, Book 1, by R. Smith, Smith Publications, Marquette, MI, 1994. 125pp., illus.

Great Michigan Deer Tales, Book 2, by R. Smith, Smith Publications, Marquette, MI, 1998. 128pp., illus.

Deer Hunting, by R. Smith, Stackpole Books, Harrisburg, PA 1978. 224 pp., illus.

Hunting Mature Bucks, by Larry L. Weishuhn, Krause Publications, Iola, WI, 1995, 256 pp., illus.

Hunting Trophy Deer, by John Wootters, The Lyons Press, New York, NY, 1997. 272pp., illus.

Hunting Trophy Whitetails, by David Morris, Stoneydale Press, Stevensville, MT, 1993. 483 pp., illus.

The Rifles, the Cartridges, and the Game, by Clay Harvey, Stackpole Books, Harrisburg, PA, 1991. 254 pp., illus.

Camp Log – Biggest Buck

(by hunter & year)

Twenty-nine years of hunting PHC

2000————Geoff Quick (8 pointer)
1999————Wayne Coston (8 pointer)
1998————Bob Mills (7 pointer)
1997————Jim Ward, Jr. (8 pointer)
1996————Joe Mills (8 pointer)
1995————Bert Palmer (13 pointer)
1994————Al Quick (8 pointer)
1993————Jamie Dixon (8 pointer)
1992————Joe Pope (8 pointer)
1991————Joe Pope (8 pointer)
1990————Larry Smiley (8 pointer)
1989————Bob Mills (9 pointer)
1988————Ron Williams (10 pointer)
1987————Mike Carey (8 pointer)
1986————Dave Mills (10 pointer)
1985————Bob Mills (8 pointer)
1984————Joe Mills (7 pointer)
1983————Dave Mills (8 pointer)
1982————Bob Caltrider (8 pointer)
1981————Rick Mills (7 pointer)
1980————Joe Mills (8 pointer)
1979————Al Quick (8 pointer)
1978————Dave Mills (8 pointer)
1977————Bob Mills (8 pointer)
1976————Dave Mills (10 pointer)
1975————Dick Kolaja (12 pointer)
1974————Joe Blackmer (10 pointer)
1973————Al Quick (8 pointer)
1972 ————Al Quick (8 pointer)

DEER HUNTER CHECKLIST

The following checklist can be used in preparing for your next deer-hunting trip.

Other items could be added but this list highlights the essentials of your equipment needs. I hope this list is helpful in planning your trip to deer camp.

1. LICENSE	19. Binoculars	37. Film
2. Rifle	20. Rainwear	38. Tow rope
3. Ammo	21. Shovel	39. Water jug
4. Knife	22. Knife sharpener	40. Scope covers
5. Socks	23. Matches/Lighter	41. Good book
6. Belt	24. Insect repellent	42. Tool kit
7. Gloves	25. Alarm clock	43. Medication
8. Hat	26. Cards	44. First aid kit
9. Jacket	27. Maps	45. Rubber gloves
10. Boots	28. Vinyl tarp	46. Bow
11. Pants	29. Lantern & fuel	47. Arrows
12. Flashlight	30. Camera	48. Quiver
13. Sleeping bag	31. Ax & saw	49. Bow case
14. Cleaning kit	32. Hand warmer	50. Sight pins
15. Back pack	33. Extra batteries	51. Sharp broad heads
16. Water bottle	34. Compass	52. Extra bow string
17. Binoculars	35. Gun case	53. Tent
18. Underwear	36. Pillow	54. Sun glasses

PALACE IN THE POPPLE

It's a smoky, raunchy boars' nest
With an unswept, drafty floor
And pillowticking curtains
And knife scars on the door.
The smell of a pine-knot fire
From a stovepipe that's come loose
Mingles sweetly with the bootgrease
And the Copenhagen snoose.

There are work-worn .30-30s
With battered, steel-shod stocks,
And drying lines of longjohns
And of steaming, pungent socks.
There's a table for the Bloody Four
And their game of two-card draw,
And there's deep and dreamless sleeping
On bunk ticks stuffed with straw.

Jerry and Jake stand by the stove,
Their gun-talk loud and hot,
And bogie has drawn a pair of kings
And is raking in the pot.
Frank's been drafted again as cook
And is peeling some spuds for stew
While Bruce wanders by in baggy drawers
Reciting "Dan McGrew."

No where on earth is fire so warm
Nor coffee so infernal,
Nor whiskers so stiff, jokes so rich,
Nor hope blooming so eternal.
A man can live for a solid week
In the same old underbritches
And walk like a man and spit when he wants
And scratch himself where he itches.

I tell you, boys, there's no place else
Where I'd rather be, come fall,
Where I eat like a bear and sing like a wolf
And feel like I'm bull-pine tall.
In that raunchy cabin out in the bush
In the land of the raven and loon,
With a tracking snow lying new to the ground
At the end of the Rutting Moon.

From the White-Tailed Deer by John Madson